Making Money Make Money

OR

A Primer of Investing

By H. L. BARBER
Economist and Financial Writer

Money makes money, and
the money that money
makes, makes more money.
—Benjamin Franklin.

CHICAGO
A. J. MUNSON & CO.
1920

Sincerely,
H. L. Barber

PREFACE

During the last dozen years I have edited and published a monthly publication in which I have advocated organized industrial and financial activity by the people for their profit, in opposition to the system that has prevailed of the people turning their savings over to the entrenched exploiting class for the latter's gain.

During these years this work received the ardent support of many hundreds of thousands of persons in the substantial walks of life, of those who are the real creators of wealth, but who, under the operation of the entrenched system, had been led to believe that it was not for them to participate justly in the wealth their labor and savings created.

The awakening that this work caused, and the assistance that it received from abler men, who, while approaching the subject from different angles, gave momentum to the force that had been applied, has found fruition in establishing throughout the country a network of industrial enterprises, owned by the people as small investors, and returning profits to them instead of to the exploiting class.

It may be understood without indicating it, that in the ratio of the people adopting and profiting by this work, the financial interests, that had become entrenched through the subornation of press, platform and pulpit and the subordination of legislative, executive and judicial branches of our governing systems, became hostile. A propaganda that promised to divert the people's money from the use of these interests, and put it at work where it would return to its owners all that it earned in profits, and not mere savings or bond interest, as before, could not be expected to be viewed complacently.

Nevertheless, the work has gone forward. Industrial enterprises have been established. Reforms in the institutions of the entrenched classes have been started and made to produce results that have proved beneficial to the people. A score of far-reaching movements for the greater welfare of the people must be credited to the work of the last decade. And the best of all is that the conscience of the public has been awakened and its intelligence directed into channels that can lead only to greater results in the years to come.

During these years I received requests to arrange the writings that contained the fundamental facts of my argument and publish them in book form, that the argument might be presented in a continuous and harmonious way for convenient reading and preservation. These requests became so numerous and insistent that I concluded to accede to them. The result is this book.

It is unnecessary to say that no effort at fine writing has been made. We who believe in the theory that the mass of the people, as opposed to the class, has some rights that should be advocated, do not care to waste time in "turning pretty phrases." The rugged truth nestles down closer to the understanding when told in the simple vernacular of everyday life—of the shop, the field, the mine.

Neither has any effort been made to avoid repeating in the different discourses what I consider to be fundamental facts in the argument. Each discourse is designed to approach the subject from a different angle, but to carry the primary truths as the base of the argument. Several ideas will, therefore, crop out again and again throughout the book, although the wording of their statement may be somewhat different.

If you have not given the subject here dealt with any consideration, and if you will read these crude pages thoughtfully and conscientiously, I believe you will come to agree with me; and, if so, you will arise from their perusal better fortified to go forward and achieve that financial success that is the source of much human happiness, and to which, in laying the foundation of the earth, a good Creator gave us a supposedly inalienable birthright.

Satan got into Eden. The exploiter got into finance and industry. Misery resulted in both instances. Only by presenting a solid front to the common enemy can he be overcome.

Let's learn to do this.

H. L. Barber.

Wheaton, Ill., March 1, 1916.

CONTENTS.

INTRODUCTION

One of our keenest national experts has said: "I don't believe that it is putting it too strongly to say that 90 per cent of the American people are only a year away from the poorhouse, and 50 per cent of them are not more than a week away from it."

Students of political economy will know that this expert, far from putting the matter too strongly, spoke with the greatest conservatism.

Mr. Thomas A. Davis, in his work, "How to Make Money," cites the example of a Boston bank which had occasion to trace out its old accounts and ascertain the history of its depositors, thus bringing to light the startling fact that of one thousand accounts, opened when the bank started, but six remained, the owners of the lapsed accounts having either failed or died destitute of property.

Roughly speaking, 95 per cent of the total population die poor, and 5 per cent die rich. Against this observe that the United States AS A WHOLE has progressed marvelously, the national wealth being in 1850, $7,135,780,000, and in 1915 (estimated), $187,739,071,090.

Let us individualize the nation as a great mother with some hundred million children, and the striking fact will be observed that there has been great favoritism in the distribution of wealth and comfort and happiness to her children; ninety-five million have little or nothing between themselves and the poorhouse; five million have a great deal; a percentage of those five million are stupendously wealthy.

Observe with this another great fact, stated by Mr. Joseph E. Davis:

"There are 305,000 corporations in the United States. Of these 296,000 have a capital, surplus and undivided profits of one million dollars or less. Only 1,600 corporations are capitalized at five million or over. But while the number of big businesses is so small, out of the 1,600 one hundred own one-seventh of the total property value of the nation.

"In other words, while 95 per cent of the business interests of the country is relatively small, the power of the few is so relatively great that if it is used unscrupulously, it menaces the opportunity of a greater number."

When these figures are contemplated it becomes evident that the wealth created by ALL the people of the United States is, by some mysterious process or principle, passing into the hands of a very FEW of our people.

Possibly nothing can be better here than to quote a very thoughtful article by Mr. John D.

Barry, that appeared in the New York Telegram:

"In school, when I first heard of the way workmen fought against the introduction of machinery, I felt very superior. I was amused at this exhibition of folly, exactly as the teacher expected us to be.

"It seemed plain to me that machinery had been invented to help the whole world. In such provision I generously included the workmen of the world.

"What half truths the children are taught in schools! They may even be more misleading than untruths. So many of them are 'warm', as we used to say. In relation to the truth we get near, but not near enough to be set free.

"Lately I have tried to picture to myself the state of mind of the workmen of the world when they first heard of the iron monsters that were to do their work so much more quickly than themselves, so much more effectually.

"In thousands of little homes there must have been consternation.

"Perhaps it was the tears of the women that led so many of the workmen in England to destroy those machines.

"Of course, it made no difference whether the workmen destroyed the machines or not. They were confronted by a force they couldn't destroy.

"An idea had got into the mind of man. It could never be dislodged. Inexorably it would do its work. Though all the machinery in the world might be destroyed, machinery would yet persist, because machinery was the idea.

"But the workmen did not go far enough in their resistance to discover for themselves the inexorable law of industrial progress. They yielded hopelessly, despairingly.

"Perhaps they would have made a harder fight if they had known that the machines were to become something worse than their rivals, their masters.

"Perhaps some of them did know.

"Yes, some of them must have known.

"There must have been prophets among them, ordinary-looking, ill-clad men like thousands of the workmen we see trudging along the street after the day's work.

"It took a long time for the men shackled to the machines to realize that they were slaves. Many of them, after becoming used to their condition, inclined to the views of the owners of machinery. They thought the owners were kind to give them work. It enabled them to exist in the world and to maintain dependent women and children. It seemed natural to them and right that they themselves should always be on the edge of want and destruction.

"It was perfectly simple:

"The owners of the machines owned the machinery.

"Of course, you see their blunder.

"Like those first workmen who tried to destroy machines, they confused machines with the IDEA behind the machines, the invention, the revelation of God to men that the burden of labor might be EASIER and that there might be INCREASE in the bounty of the earth.

"They could not see it was the capture by the few of this revelation that had turned them into slaves, working for just enough to keep them out of want and death.

"Many see now. And they are trying to make others see. The task is not easy. Our vision becomes blurred from the habit of looking at things in the old, conventional ways.

"But the time is coming when we shall all see."

Divine Providence has dowered America with marvelous wealth through its farms and mines and fisheries, its forests and inventions and industries. It has conferred this wealth on the people of America as their birthright and heritage.

will simply ask guidance as to the right way to accomplish the end sought.

It ought not to be very difficult to regard the things that are on this earth, and the things that come on it like flashes of thought that crystalize into machines and other things, as the gifts of God to his children that people the earth.

Newell Dwight Hillis once said:

"If we examine the tendencies of invention and the mechanical arts, we shall find that even tools have become evangelists, and machines prophets of a new day. From every voice come voices foretelling an age of wealth and happiness and comfort. Every time a river is enslaved a thousand men are set free. Every time an iron wheel is mastered a thousand human muscles are emancipated."

A new day may indeed be coming, but it is not here yet; when a river is enslaved a thousand muscles OUGHT to be set free, but they are not. "The iron wheel" does NOT emancipate a thousand human muscles—they are led to toil elsewhere. We still have with us the hopelessly outclassed clerk of forty-five or fifty, "a week from the poorhouse," industriously getting ready to die poor.

The world is getting richer and richer; inventions FORETELL an ideal as yet not reached; the PROMISE of things as they are is roseate

DISCOURSE I.

MASTERING THE ART OF MONEY-MAKING.

The man who would build a fortune must learn the difference between the EARNING POWER of money and the RENTAL VALUE of money.

The sooner he learns this the sooner he will accomplish his purpose.

The RENT paid for the use of money is necessarily much less than the EARNING POWER of money, because the rent must be paid out of the earnings and leave a balance as a profit for the borrower—the one who employs the borrowed money to earn more money. It is almost invariably true that the earning power of any certain amount of money is several times the amount paid for the use, or rent, of a similar amount of money.

Therefore it is manifest that the one who wishes to build his fortune as rapidly as possible must use his money at its FULL EARNING CAPACITY. This is done by engaging in business on his own account, or either with a partner or partners, or in the form of a corporation. The latter is the most favorable, and is rapidly becoming the most generally adopted.

Men with small or large means engage in business through corporations by investing in their capital stock, thereby holding a proportional share of the assets, and sharing similarly in the profits of the business.

Money, to earn the maximum of its power, must necessarily be engaged in a CREATIVE capacity, and not in a PASSIVE one as it is when rented or hired out. It should not be expected that the hired man's earnings are as great as those of his employer.

It is evident that young men and men of small means, who may desire to build fortunes, must INVEST their money, which means that they must put it at work in a CREATIVE way so it may EARN TO THE LIMIT OF ITS CAPACITY. In so doing a certain amount of risk is necessarily entailed, as all great and valuable achievements and gains have resulted or been accomplished only through the taking of risks—sometimes great ones.

If such a principle as limiting one's profits to a savings bank rate—the elimination of all speculation from enterprises—had been rigidly enforced in America the last hundred years, but little development would have resulted. We would not now be connected by rail with the Pacific coast, and our rich central and western domain, would still be a wilderness.

DISCOURSE I.

Pioneering in the field of finance, with its attendant risks, must offer large prospective profits, or why should one chance them?

For old men, and rich men, those ready to retire from the burdens of life, the lending of money is often the better plan. If their money is rented out, or loaned to successful and financially responsible men or corporations, they will have a higher degree of safety and convertibility, and an income of from three to six per cent—rarely more, and generally from three to five per cent.

Money rents precisely as houses rent, but the rental paid for its use is called interest.

When through wise and successful investments a man has made enough money that the interest on it will furnish him sufficient income for his needs, it is often better for him to lend his money to men or corporations that are ambitious to make money earn the limit, and who are so capable and sucessful that the return of the principal and interest thereon is assured to him.

To be sure, there are years, political economists tell us and give statistics as proof, when the purchasing power of money deteriorates more than the interest it draws. For example, there have been years recently, during the period of the high cost of living, in which the purchasing power of money has fallen more than eight per cent yearly. In such years the man with money rented at, say, five per cent, has actually lost not only his interest, but three per cent of his principal as well. It does not require much of a financier to figure out how many years it would take the principal rented out under such conditions to disappear entirely.

The average cost of living has increased about fifty per cent during the last twenty years. The man who put $1,000 into a 20-year bond twenty years ago will receive $1,000 now when the bond falls due, but this $1,000 will now buy only half as much as it did twenty years ago. He has, therefore, lost half his principal. In the meantime this money has not been producing any more, year by year, than it did twenty years ago, and each successive year the interest he received has had a lesser purchasing power.

This is one of the problems that confront America today, for the cost of living is mounting higher and higher, which means that the purchasing power of money is falling lower and lower, while the rental value of money remains practically stationary with a tendency to move downward.

Generally speaking, the great fortunes of America were made by men who were ambitious to make fortunes, who took the risks that attend all investing, and who, by courage and good judgment, put their money actively at work in enterprises and industries that offered the largest returns on the money invested—who planted their money in rich industrial soil, as the farmer plants his seed in fertile ground with the assurance of a bountiful harvest. Properly invested or planted dollars have always earned, and always will, many dollars, a harvest of money profits.

There has, however, crept into our economy a plan whereby combinations of rich and influential men borrow the money of great numbers of people who are afraid to invest their money and make it work for them. With the enormous aggregate so controlled these men make gigantic investments and reap correspondingly great profits, so that the three or five per cent they pay the timid owners of the money for the use of it, when deducted from the large earnings, leaves tremendous profits for the men who borrowed the money as a reward for their ability and judgment.

"The dictionaries say a capitalist is a person who supplies capital", observes Will Irwin in the Saturday Evening Post. "But the dictionaries are quite wrong. A real capitalist is a person who gets other people to supply capital, while he controls the enterprise and secures a large share of the profits.''

These methods account for many of the great American fortunes. The plan of borrowing the people's money for a pittance became so successful and popular that, to get more of it—to get all of it—and further to have a monopoly of investing money in the best creative enterprises, a combination of the great borrowers was formed to create the general belief that money could no longer be employed safely at good profits—in short, that from three per cent to five per cent was all that money could earn with safety. They laid great stress on ''safety'' arguing that no man of small means should ever INVEST his money, but should always LEND it, and lend it to those who had become enormously rich, through the earnings of the people's money, that the money loaned would be ''safe''.

To give color and credence to this strange and false doctrine, great newspapers and magazines were employed to preach it continually to the people. College professors were paid to teach it to the youth, and even ministers to expound it from the pulpit. All avenues for the dissemination of information and the spreading of knowledge were monopolized to the end that the people should forever forget the true value of their money, and thus be content to spend their lives in drudgery, skimping and hoarding that the money borrowers might have the enormous total of the people's small sums to use for their own great profit.

To make it easier to carry out this scheme, which leads inevitably to the enslavement of the people, in reality if not in semblance, the influential publications of the country were caused to give great prominence to all unsuccessful attempts of men to build up enterprises and thereby to lead the people to the false belief that the making of money is attended by great risks; that only a chosen few can do so successfully.

In the same way the people of the earth were once taught, and finally convinced for centuries, that they were incompetent to govern themselves, and that only a certain set of men, styled kings, could govern successfully. This deception was carried to the extent that these self-appointed kings declared that they derived their powers from God, and even in this alleged enlightened age the Money Kings—the Royal Rulers of the Empire of Capital—claim not only a divine right to the people's savings, but go so far as to assert that the coal, iron, gold, oil and other resources of the earth were deposited not for the people of the earth, but for the "elect"—these self-appointed Royal Rulers who flourish and draw their substance and their increment from the people — through the apathy, ignorance and superstition of the people.

That this is a true statement of conditions as they actually are today, no one who has studied well and thought deeply can deny. These conditions are the crux of the present great wave of political unrest. They are the cause of the rapidly rising tide of economic discontent which on all sides is admitted to be urging America to a revolution which may or may not be bloodless.

That the people—the great and overwhelming majority against which nothing human can stand when it is aroused—will remain in this bondage until they throw off superstition and emerge from the swamp of ignorance into which they have unconsciously permitted themselves to be led, cannot be denied. The only way for them to regain their freedom and secure their birthright is to cast away from the old traditions, cut loose from the fetters by which they are bound, and assert themselves as free men, competent to do their own thinking, their own governing, and manage their own affairs under the same natural laws and in accordance with the same principles that have enabled their masters to gain the mastery.

When that day arrives there will be a new era, a haven of prosperity for those who deserve; for then they will set their own money to work for themselves; they will make it earn the limit in enterprises that are useful to humanity, and the profits will flow to the natural owners—those who always have furnished and always will furnish the money to do the work of the world.

Then investing, not lending, will be the royal road to wealth for ALL, as it has been for a FEW; and only the rich and the old who want to retire from life's activities will be content to LEND their money, and there will be established such safeguards that men of capacity and integrity, though possessed of small means, may share in the USE of their money for their own and their fellows' welfare.

The first lesson necessary to be learned in this course of progress is the one that teaches the difference between the EARNING POWER and the RENTAL VALUE of money.

DISCOURSE II.

SECRET OF FORTUNE BUILDING.

I see in the future a crisis approaching that unnerves me and causes me to tremble for the safety of my country. As a result of war, corporations have been enthroned and an era of corruption in high places will follow, and the money power of the country will endeavor to prolong its reign until all wealth is concentrated in a few hands and the republic is destroyed.—From a letter written by Abraham Lincoln, November 21, 1864.

Wealth has its origin in natural resources. A thing is not wealth unless it is useful. To make a natural resource useful usually requires work. To get work done requires wealth. The process of producing wealth becomes, then, an endless chain, beginning and ending in wealth.

You and I want wealth, at least a sufficient amount to make us and those depending on us reasonably comfortable.

Now, of which link in this wealth-producing chain do you and I form a part?

If we have some wealth we can set it to work to produce more. We can do this either by organizing a wealth-producing business of our own and managing it, or we can invest our wealth in a business managed by someone else and become sharers in the profits in proportion to the interest we own in it.

If we have no wealth we must work for someone who has. But no one ever acquired enough by working for others to entitle the amount to be called wealth. The supply of workers is too great, and they are too poorly organized socially to get very much more than a scant living in return for what they give.

Yet nearly every man who has acquired great wealth began as a worker for others. Rockefeller was a grocer's clerk, Carnegie an office boy, Vanderbilt a deck hand, Gould a surveyor's helper, Marshall Field a dry goods clerk, Pullman a house mover's helper, McCormick a farm hand, Hearst a miner, and so on down the line.

When these men started in life they had only the ability to do a day's work, the same as you and I. They saw, as you and I have seen, that this in and of itself would not get them wealth. They had the self-denial to save some of their earnings and the courage to set their savings at work to earn money.

All human experience teaches that it is wise to follow a good example. You and I have before us today just as good opportunities as these men had. The only question that remains, then, is, have we the courage to make use of them?

In beginning a career of acquiring wealth it is necessary to understand a few fundamental principles.

The first is that money has an EARNING POWER and a RENTAL VALUE, and that this power and this value are not the same thing.

The second is that there are degrees in the earning power and rental value of money.

Money may be set at work by either lending it or investing it.

Money is loaned when it draws a fixed rate of interest. It is invested when it shares equitably in all the profits it earns.

Putting money into notes, mortgages, bonds and savings banks is giving it a RENTAL VALUE. Investing it as capital in an enterprise is giving it an EARNING POWER. The rental value is represented by INTEREST; the earning power by profits, or DIVIDENDS.

The rental value of money is always small, because it is only a part of its earning power. The person who borrows it does so to put it at work where it will have an earning power. Out of the proceeds of this earning power he pays the lender the interest agreed on, and keeps the remainder for himself.

Only those who have much money can afford to put it at work for its rental value. Those who have but little money must put it at work where they will receive its full earning power, if they desire to become wealthy.

Putting money in the savings bank at 3 per cent, or in bonds at from 3 per cent to 5 per cent, or in mortgages at from 5 per cent to 6 per cent, is too slow a process for the person who has but a few hundred or thousand dollars. A lifetime of this will not amount to much.

On the other hand, if he puts it at work where he receives its full earning power of 25 per cent, 100 per cent, or, as is frequently the case, 1,000 per cent, and then puts the earnings at work in a similar way, he may expect to get into comfortable circumstances in a few years.

There are today innumerable opportunities for money to have a tremendous earning power—where its earning power is from 100 per cent to 1,000 per cent or more.

An average thrifty person should be able to save at least $100 a year. If he saves that amount each year for ten years and at the end of each year puts his savings and the money these savings earn at work where his money will have an earning power of only 100 per cent, at the end of the ten years he will have $82,300. If he continues the process five years longer he will be a multimillionaire.

It is this process that makes millionaires. Men become wealthy through the earning power of money, not through its rental value. The person who saves $100 a year and puts it in a savings bank to draw 3 per cent interest, or buys bonds that draw 5 per cent, will have to live many lifetimes to become a millionaire.

He who has but little money, or who can save only a few dollars a year, rarely finds an opportunity to use the little money he has in organizing a business enterprise of his own and managing it. To make money with his money he must, therefore, join his money with that of others until they get enough together to finance the proposed enterprise.

To enable small investors to finance large enterprises for their mutual profit, the corporation was evolved. On this plan great numbers of persons may engage in business by investing their money in shares of stock and elect a few persons to manage their business for them. This plan gives the advantage of a large capital and the greatest economy in the transaction of the business. It is the ideal way for the person who has but little money to engage in business where his money will have an earning power.

In buying stock in a corporation the person who has but little money to invest should seek a line of industry where his money will have the greatest possible earning power. Unless he does this he cannot hope to become wealthy from his small investments.

It follows also that he should secure an interest in such a corporation as near the beginning of the developing period of the corporation's industry as possible, when stock may usually be had at a low price. In this way he will gain wealth through the increasing value of his stock as well as in the dividends when the profit producing period is reached.

By following this plan it usually does not require very many years for him to accumulate enough to retire from the hazards of business, if he desires, by selling his stocks at high prices, and put his money at work at a rental value with good security. If he has accumulated enough through the earning power of his money its rental value will then be sufficient to supply his wants without taking any business risks.

The usual investor, broker or financier looks through the glass of rental value when he inspects an investment opportunity, or is considering the money-earning power of any enterprise. If he is considering a share of stock he invariably compares it erroneously with the evidence of some loan, a certificate of deposit, a bond or a note.

He wants to know what it is worth. He asks: "What can I get for it today in money?" and similar questions bearing entirely upon its present market value. He forgets that investments are made entirely for the future, and not for the present; that the real value of any true investment lays before and not behind; that the desirability of an investment is determined by the future earnings that may possibly be very large, and not by what the security may earn today. He sees only the present.

The rental value of money is determined today, and today only is concerned with it. A good loan, or renting out of money, is nothing if it does not bring today, now, a proper amount in rent or interest with which to meet today's expenses and requirements.

The ordinary man who poses as an advisor of investors asks for convertibility, forgetting that loans only are convertible. No investment is convertible save those which, by reason of a compound nature, may possess as well the features of a loan.

Such a man will class as worthless, or of small account, a share of stock that will not immediately SELL FOR as large a sum as was exchanged for it for investment purposes. He will often condemn such a security in spite of the fact that in the future, as is frequently the case, it may pay to its possessor in earned profits dividends amounting to several hundred or several thousand times as much as the same sum of money could have been loaned for and been in the position of immediate convertibility.

If you invest $1,000 today in some business opportunity to make large profits from the workable combination of courage, good judgment and profit opportunity, you cannot and will not expect to get your money back with large profits unless you, too, "stay with it" to the end.

Having made such an investment and desiring to drop it and get your money back, you will find that the re-sale of the evidence of your ownership, the stock certificate, will have to be made to another in much the same way you would sell a horse, or any other personal property. To get a good price for it you will have to find a purchaser who has the same faith in it that you have. If you do not do that, you will resort to brokers, who, unfortunately, are engaged in buying and selling LOANS, not INVESTMENTS. Their only view of your stock certificate is what they could sell it for NOW, and that price is inevitably determined by what it brings in now, each year, in the form of dividends, which they consider as rent or interest.

A bond is not an investment, it is a loan; so with a note, or a preferred share of stock.

It is hoped that the difference between earnings and rent is now clear. If you want CONVERTIBILITY, you don't want INVESTMENT, for you can get convertibility only through loans, for they only concern the present. To get convertibility you will want to buy a bond or a note, or shares of preferred stock, proper evidences of money loaned.

However, if you want to make money quickly and as rapidly as old Earth's best opportunities will permit, you will not seek convertibility for the present, but investment for the future. Convertibility will then take care of itself in due time.

And here lies, to a great measure, the secret of fortune. The world is blessed, in a way, because there are so many timid people; so many who are afraid to take a legitimate chance by engaging in business through investment, thereby leaving room for those ambitious souls, who, stout of heart and wiser than their fellows, put their money and energies into the development or promotion of some plan or scheme that brings to them a practical monopoly over the wants of their fellowmen, and who, from their timid neighbors, reap tremendous profits for themselves.

Such is investment—fruit plucked from dizzy heights, or difficult places, where the many fear to go, and converted into immense profits from the very ones who would rather surrender their daily pittance for these very fruits, than with fortitude and courage seek them for themselves.

Well may Herbert Kauffman, the "business philosopher", say:

"The best way to GET a CHANCE is to TAKE ONE. When you strike a CERTAINTY, you strike LIMITATIONS. The MAKING of PROFITS almost always means the TAKING OF RISK."

Had the first John Jacob Astor been contented to toil and slave and merely lend his money there would have been no stupendous Astor fortune to distinguish the name and enable his posterity to enjoy affluence, ease and power.

Had Andrew Carnegie invested his savings in bonds, or preferred stocks drawing a certain interest, but interest only—had he LOANED his money, he would not have become one of the country's richest men and its most consistent philanthropist.

DISCOURSE II.

Had John D. Rockefeller been merely a hoarder and lender of money, the country might yet be paying many times the present prices for lubricants and illuminants, and the "Oil King" might have been a very commonplace business man instead of the financial colossus, the marvel of all ages.

Had Gould or Vanderbilt or Hill merely loaned their money, the railroad development that has been the backbone of American progress might still be in a primitive stage, and their fortunes and the comfort and respect these bring to such founders and their families and associates, only mediocre.

Whatever may be said of these men and of the industries they created and the resources they cultivated, they have, by their works, been world builders—greater than Napoleons; for aside from their fortunes, the benefits they have endowed upon humanity have created for them enduring niches in history which time nor calumny—not even corruption and abuse of privileges—can efface. Their good actions will live, even after the injustices arising from abused wealth have been rectified and forgotten.

Then all hail to the Opportunist! Hail to those wise and brave souls who, seeing a chance, took a chance, thereby rising to affluence and ease in their old age. Their wealth, and the power that wealth honorably won always brings, is shared in by millions of their fellow men, to the enrichment and contentment of all.

When once our people have learned the significance of the difference between the earning power of money and its rental value, and they have acted upon that knowledge, a new era will have dawned in our economic history. The oft-repeated admonition of the Money Trust to our toiling millions: "Slave and save that you may lend to us," will go unheeded. Instead of lending their billions of hard-earned savings to the principals and beneficiaries of the Money Trust they will put their money at work for themselves, and the tremendous profits and unlimited power now controlled by the few will be shared in by all, by the REAL owners.

And in no longer "slaving and saving" that they may LEND their money to the "money ring", they will forever break the chains of bondage forced upon them by the Royal Rulers of the Empire of Capital, and themselves become founders and enjoy the great profits and the power of successful founders.

And thus the reign of the Royal Rulers will cease, for no longer will they be able to manipulate the people's billions to perpetuate the people's bondage, now made possible by the ignorance of the victims of their teachings, that no one but the elect should invest, but LEND, and lend to them, the Royal Rulers, and for their aggrandizement and unlimited power—an advantage they possess because they know the value of money and its power; because they are INVESTORS, not LENDERS, and because their gigantic investments are made possible only by borrowing for a pittance the billions of the people's savings.

Manifestly, the way to wealth is only along the broad highway of investment, where OPPORTUNITY ever lurks, and not by a narrow lane of money lending whose end is either a blind alley or a trackless desert.

DISCOURSE III.

INVESTMENT—THE WAY TO FORTUNE.

It is a saying as old as the race that "fortune favors the bold."

Note these words and particularly the word BOLD.

What is "boldness"? Boldness does not mean foolishness, imprudence, recklessness. Boldness means to "PLAN with COURAGE". Look in the good old dictionary of the English language and SEE. Boldness, to be "manful". Boldness means "strong hearted" and "confident".

Now if you will note that these qualities are the attributes of ALL SUCCESS, the words of the old maxim will shine forth in the light of their true meaning—you will get a glimpse of the ANSWER to the question suggested by FINANCIAL SUBORDINATION and SUBSERVIENCY.

There is a tremendous lesson in the rise of German industry.

The German people believed in and backed one another. This is the secret of German success in manufacture, in invention and in perfection of processes, improvements, devices, methods, machinery, etc. The German Government itself, unlike any other except that of Russia, did more before the war to foster and promote INDIVIDUAL BUSINESS ENTERPRISE than was ever done previously in the history of the world.

It was the German Government, competing directly with the industries of France, that fostered the manufacture of fine silks, laces and the various fabrics used in making women's wear. New machines were devised, companies formed. The Government took stock, the people bought shares. They were not afraid to trust one another and to help in the upbuilding of an industrial strength. They were taught to invest their money in the work of others than themselves. They were not taught to put their money into bonds issued by borrowers of bond money, who in their turn reap the harvest.

It is no misstatement to assert that the vast majority of the fortunes made by Americans are made by PLANNING BOLDLY, of having a decent respect for the enterprise, ingenuity, energy, diligence and integrity of their business neighbors.

The German genius learned early to TAKE STOCK. The Frenchman has been an inveterate buyer of bonds. FRANCE STOOD STILL. Germany transcended all expectations, until her commercial and industrial triumph threatened to dominate the world.

France LOANED on BONDS—Germany INVESTED in STOCKS. This is true everywhere. The best investments in America (despite the statement of R. G. Dun that 95 per cent of all business ventures result in failure), are investments in the stocks of companies, conservatively organized, honestly conducted, ably managed and BOLDLY PLANNED.

Incidentally we have an impression that the above undoubted statements of Dun and Bradstreet are misleading. Dun's summary includes every little store and shop, every little millinery, every grocery, started up in town and village — every misguided business hope, chanced by people unprepared and unqualified—women going into business for themselves backed by a little life insurance, young fellows starting up prematurely, even against the advice of friends;—and therefore it would seem that the great sweeping statement of 95 per cent of failures was unjustified, IN THIS SENSE.

Let us look in the strong box of the banker. What will we find there? Bonds only? No, and again NO! Stocks, stocks in scores of businesses, splendid investments in institutions that have grown from littleness until today they are POWERS in their respective fields—and paying princely dividends.

How many bankers inherited their banks? If they did not inherit them, how got they the money that lifted them to their presidencies?

Turn to the histories of the prominent men in your state, your county or city, and read the records of the rich!

They PLANNED BOLDLY and fortune favored them. They invested their dollars in DEEDS—in the DOING of THINGS—not in bonds. Business grew and flourished. They made money hand over fist. They accumulated wealth; wealth lifted them into the realm of finance—and behold your bank president.

This is true in the city of Chicago in scores of cases. It is true in New York city, true in St. Louis, true in Philadelphia, true in the smaller cities, true even in the little towns. Look about you and study your millionaire in the making, and observe the same development. He couldn't afford to lend his money at 3 per cent, and, what's more, HE DIDN'T. The money has to WORK for him. He put it into the mill and the factory, the shop, the laboratory, the patent, the invention, the store, and the mine. He had faith in his fellows. He was not a subscriber to the fallacy that "all men are liars."

He had faith to believe—he trusted his fellow-men. He is doing it every day. Whom do you know that is making money? How? Where? Why? Is his money in bonds, or is it "hard-at-it" in the busy hands of honest men?

I protest against the propaganda that would teach the toiler to slave for his money and then bury it. I protest against the monstrous wrong of preaching to the world the doctrine of SLAVE and SAVE. Slave if you must, but give your money a chance.

Slave if you must to earn what you can—but in the name of common sense, put what you save to WORK.

Down in the city of Atlanta was one man who had faith in the future of an idea and a thing. He had a few friends, and they were small, too, in the money sense. But they stood by him with the little they could afford, trusted him and his ability and his idea—and he made them rich. The stock they took against the advice of bank and banker, financiers and friends—today pays princely dividends. It is Coca Cola.

Two men who planned boldly came out from Massachusetts to St. Louis. They believed that shoes could be manufactured in the West as well as in the East, and sold to the people of the West at prices that would mean business.

They started. They formed a little company. They began at the beginning. A few took stock.

Another little group of men followed who also planned boldly.

Today St. Louis is the shoe mart of the world. The shoe industry of St. Louis is a mother of millionaires.

Meantime there have been failures in the beverage business and in the shoe business—yes, MANY, perhaps. But the proposition stands. AND INVESTMENTS STAND. Money at work for you on stock of your own is better than money loaned by you on bonds to make profits on stocks for somebody else.

It has been said by one of the most successful men in this country, "I made my money BACKING BRAINS. I do not win all the time, but I win some of the time—AND WHEN I DO WIN I WIN BIG."

There are scores of opportunities open to the American investor right under his nose. A hundred dollars, five hundred dollars, or a thousand dollars put into a business in its infancy, its formative stage—just getting started—where dollars help and help big, may not all prove to be Coca Colas or bank presidents, but SOME of them will grow—and grow great. The man who has one thousand dollars only should not invest it all in one thing—never. There are as big fish in the sea as ever were caught. Let him invest $200 of his $1,000; let the $800 wait. Other opportunities will come. Divide the risk. Plan boldly—but learn the rule of percentage.

The executors of E. H. Harriman threw out huge sums of poor investments he had made, yet his estate had piled up to a hundred million. There were plenty of "undigested securities" in the strong box of J. P. Morgan. The Vanderbilts have made mistakes. Russell Sage was not infallible. The Rothschilds had their losses. But in the division of the risks, by investing to the best of their ability—by PLANNING BOLDLY—investing some here and some there when opportunity arrived, fortune favored them.

Even as this is being written the announcement is made of the cutting of a profit sharing melon by the Ford Motor Company at Detroit. The amount of it is $15,000,000. It occurs to me, by way of commentary, that certain ultra-conservative and over-cautious persons (still living) in another city where Henry Ford's "idea" went begging, and where they preferred to put their money into bonds rather than into "Henry's STOCK", may be in a position to dwell eloquently on this subject of "INVESTMENT—THE WAY TO FORTUNE."

DISCOURSE IV.

BUYING BONDS, OR "INVESTING FOR INTEREST".

Now there abideth "bonds", "speculation", and "investments"—these three—but the greatest of these is—NOT THE BOND.

Why?

Is not a bond an investment?

It is not.

Why not?

Because, according to every authority, and as stated in the "Investment Catechism", a bond is nothing in the world but "a certificate or promise to REPAY money secured by mortgage or other supposed guarantee."

The rental terms—conditions and time of return of the principal—are fixed; it is a loan, nothing but a loan—or the evidence of a loan. The money is not definitely put into the bond or anything behind the bond. It is loaned merely—not invested. When you buy a bond you buy a promissory note—you make a loan—you lend; you do NOT invest at all.

Investment is the act of buying and paying for actual ownership in the thing purchased.

The war of the rebellion popularized the coupon bond in consequence of its adoption by the Government, and made it the favorite form of bonded security. "Then", says a distinguished financier, "the railroads and other corporations lost no time in availing themselves of the CONFIDENCE which the new species of debenture inspired, and were soon flooding the country with 'bonds' carrying coupon attachments." Nor is this all, for, "except for Government and municipal uses, there never was a more disastrous or more ingenious invention. It has been the means of numberless deceptions, and has inflicted heavier losses on the investing public than all other devices combined."

Now let us see WHY. Let us look behind the veil of "security"—and behold the true inwardness of this great totem pole fetish of "safety".

The reason for the failures of bonds is just this: Being supplemental to stock issues, they have DUPLICATED representatives of the SAME values and led to excessive issues of securities based on the same properties; they have separated investors from the management and control of the identical properties into which their moneys have gone; and, being based on mortgages promising absolute security and safety, they have too often accomplished the grossest deceptions. In short, a bond is the financial counterpart of "taxation without representation."

Money has two powers—its LOAN power and its FULL EARNING power. In the first case you "hire out" your money for another to work it, just as an employee rents himself to his employer at a fixed wage scale. In the other—which is investment in the true and only sense—you give your money its freedom to exert itself to its utmost and you take all the profit—the same as a man who goes into business for himself—works his own shop—tills his own land. One is the servant, the other is master.

Bonded debts—bonds themselves—are the evidence of money rented out or loaned out to do servant's work at servant's pay under a master. Investment is the evidence of YOUR MONEY doing YOUR work for YOUR profit under YOUR control.

We do not condemn all bonds. Some bonds are good—good for the buyer as well as the seller, if sold by fair means, without misrepresentations, and bought with full knowledge, without misapprehensions. They are for two classes of lenders (erroneously called investors): First—those who want to lend or rent out their surplus funds for a definite time only; second—for those who do not want to assume the responsibility of business and the chance of varying profits that naturally attend industrial enterprises.

The man or woman interested in bonds, who is seeking to convert cash into paper under the delusion of safety, should consider the multiplicity of bonds.

By multiplying the excuses and justifications for bonds, they are manufacturing bonds by the wholesale these days. Instead of Government and municipal bonds—the original true source and security—we have today a veritable plethora—a forest of bonds—a wilderness—railroad bonds, telegraph and telephone bonds, industrial bonds, water works bonds, bridge bonds, electric bonds, steamboat bonds, apartment house bonds, yea, and even cemetery bonds.

Of the making of bonds there is no end—first and second mortgage bonds, income bonds, convertible bonds, consolidated bonds, redemption bonds, renewal bonds, terminal bonds, divisional bonds, sinking fund bonds, blanket bonds, collateral trust bonds, equipment bonds, and bonds ad nauseum, bonds upon bonds, bonds secured by bonds, until they lap and overlap in endless complications.

"But", says the banker, "these bonds are listed by the bond division of the stock exchange

—they posses intrinsic value or they would not be so listed."

Exactly; thousands of persons INFER that BECAUSE a bond is listed it has value for that reason. Yet it may have been listed in the first instance for the express purpose of creating precisely that impression, and, at the same time, make it susceptible of manipulation, not for the sake of safety, but for purposes of the rankest character of speculation.

The stock exchange is a vain thing for safety. It is the worst guide in the world for buyers. Visit its sessions and judge for yourself! A place of pandemonium—tumult—mania—a riot of traffic—a gambling house de luxe—inferno furioso! Then imagine the quality of safety possessed by bonds made in such a madhouse.

Yet, there are good bonds—bonds of the Government, bonds of solid and conservative growing municipalities not overbonded. And bonds of this honest and wholesome standard, bonds in this original sense of bonds, form ideal securities for those who have reached the period of comfortable leisure, wealth or age. But for the vigorous, the strong, the young, those whose fortunes are yet in the making—a bond is the badge of financial servitude.

The banker who recommends the bond—does he employ his own money in bonds, or the bank's money? Does the 3 to 5 per cent income on bonds build the bank's palatial building? Or is it the returns on support given the investment for profit in the busy work of men—loans and investments on and in the products and operations of industries, commercial enterprises? Which?

The value of a bond today is not the value of that bond tomorrow. The buying power of money is constantly decreasing, but the face of the bond remains the same.

Today a dollar will buy only about half as much as it did twenty years ago. It will buy even less twenty years from now.

Had you put a thousand dollars into a bond twenty years ago, maturing today, you would now get your thousand dollars—if it was a good bond—but your money would buy you only about half as much as it would have done twenty years ago. You would have lost half the value of your principal. In the meantime you kept getting no bigger interest on your bond than if the integrity of the value of your principal had been kept intact. On the other hand, had your money been INVESTED in a useful industry it would have increased in value through the increased value of its productivity.

Do you see the difference?

DISCOURSE IV.

Have you not observed the long periods of time—ten years, twenty years, fifty years, one hundred years—for which bonds are issued, "twenty-year bonds", "fifty-year bonds", etc.? Then consider what your thousand dollars will earn for the borrower of your thousand during those twenty years, fifty years. What profits he will make on the free use of your money while you fold your hands and hold your bond in the "safety" of a meagre 3 to 5 per cent.

There is no hope, no opportunity, no possible chance for any profit whatsoever on the money you lend when you take a bond, except the face of that bond and the 3 to 5 per cent rental; no participation whatsoever in the profits of those who borrow your money; no voice whatever in its management or use. Your money makes the profits—not for you but for the borrower—of 10 per cent, 20 per cent, 50 per cent, 100 per cent—even 1,000 per cent. But your part is the 3 to 5 per cent rental. They invested your money—put it at actual work—the money you might have invested.

You loaned it and took their bond. Your rent part is 5 per cent—no more. Meanwhile your security is growing old—weak; you are a mortgagee.

In other words, you are a bondholder; you hold the bond, so far as the investment is concerned. In other words, out of the financial grist you got the bran, he got the flour.

DISCOURSE V.

INVESTING, SPECULATING, GAMBLING—WHICH?

* INVEST—To lay out (money or capital) in business with the view of obtaining an income or profit; to convert into some form of wealth other than money, usually of a more or less permanent form and as a means of obtaining income or profit; as to invest money in bank stock.

—Webster's New International Dictionary.

LEND—To allow the possession and use of, on condition of the return of an equivalent in kind; as, to lend money, flour, etc.

—Webster's New International Dictionary.

SPECULATE—(Com.) To enter into a business transaction or venture from which the profits or returns are conjectural because the undertaking is out of the ordinary course of business; to purchase or sell with the expectation of profiting by anticipated, but conjectural, fluctuations in price; often, in a somewhat depreciative sense, to engage in hazardous business transactions for the chance of an unusually large profit; as, to SPECULATE in coffee, in sugar, or in bank stock.

—Webster's New International Dictionary.

GAMBLE—(1) To play or game for money or other stake, as at cards, dice, billiards, horseracing, cockfighting, etc. (2) Hence; To stake money or any other thing of value upon an uncertain event; to hazard something upon a chance; to wager; as, to GAMBLE in stocks or in wheat.

—Webster's New International Dictionary.

In my little pen talks thus far I have tried to show what is meant by investing and by lending money.

Unless those articles failed in their purpose they should have shown you, briefly stated, that when you invest money you put it at work permanently, and receive in return all that it earns; and that when you lend money you part with the use of it for a specified time, and receive in return a small annual rental called interest.

In investing you do not get back your principal, except by selling your interest in the company to someone else. Owning shares in a corporation is a form of partnership in its industry, in that it involves part ownership of the business and a proportionate sharing in its profits.

In lending money you get back your principal at the end of the lending period—if the borrower is sufficiently substantial financially to pay it back—but you do not share in the profits. All you get is a little interest. After deducting this interest, the profit your money has made goes to the borrower.

Whether you invest or lend you are taking a business risk with your money. Don't lose sight of that fact. The investment is the foundation of the business. Whatever merit the loan has rests on the stability of the investment. If the investment is not substantial, the loan is not. The building cannot be firmer than the foundation. Is it not better, then, to be an owner than a creditor? The risk, if any, is similar in both instances. But the reward is not. In success the investor gets big profits, frequently hundreds and thousands of per cent from year to year, while the lender gets his paltry 3 to 6 per cent interest—rarely more.

Now a few words about SPECULATION and GAMBLING, words that today are so misused, abused, cuffed and knocked about by financial pirates in the business world that if Noah Webster could return and observe their usage he wouldn't be able to recognize their significance.

Speculation is an estimate by rule or reason on the future rise or fall of prices. To speculate is to buy on the strength of a reasonable expectation that the price will advance so one may sell at a profit.

When you buy a piece of land to hold it for an advance on the price with the intention of selling it when the price advances, you speculate.

When you buy a piece of land to work it and raise crops for profit, you invest.

When you buy a store to sell it at an advance on the price, you speculate.

When you buy or start a store to conduct it for profit, you invest. You engage in a business venture.

When you buy a share of stock in a corporation for the purpose of selling it when the price advances, you speculate.

When you buy that share to hold it for the profits it will yield you in dividends, you invest.

That is more emphatically true when you buy the share during the corporation's formative period when your money goes to develop the business.

Speculation is legitimate enough, although when it is carried too far it comes as near gambling as it can be without being it. Speculation when founded on a mere guess or hope becomes practically gambling. Gambling is not legitimate.

With the popularization of the modern corporation a great deal of capital became invested in corporation shares, and frequently owners of these shares found themselves in financial circumstances that made it necessary for them to sell their shares.

Others who had not had the opportunity to buy treasury shares in these corporations were glad of the opportunity to buy from the shareholders.

This created a market for corporation shares, as there is a market for other commodities.

To facilitate these transactions, stock exchanges were established where the buyers and sellers could meet and exchange shares for money. Gradually this was left to their agents, called brokers.

With the development of the stock exchange came the opportunity of the schemer, the manipulator, the speculator, even the gambler. By "bearing" the price of a stock, that is, offering to buy at less than the stock was worth, some owners became frightened and sold. Frequently this resulted in heavy selling at any price offered. The speculator bought. When the selling craze died the speculator "bulled" the market, that is, offered to sell at an advanced price, and in this way gradually restored the normal price and unloaded his holding at a good profit.

The speculator's profit depended on the contingency of the price being raised. Such transactions were not considered to be conservative business. Risk and odium were attached to them, and rightly. In the popular mind they were often regarded as gambling, and quite naturally.

To handle such manipulations on large scales required tremendous volumes of money—millions and tens of millions. The further contents of this book will show how, through the savings banks, life insurances companies, bond and preferred stock issues, the pyramiding of securities and the organizing of holding companies, the capitalistic clique got possession of the people's money to be used in part in these manipulations and in part to finance industrial enterprises to the great profit of the members of the clique. Naturally the men who belong to this large clique do not want the people to retain control of their money and use it themselves.

During the last ten years there has been a great awakening among the people on financial matters, and especially on the earning power of money. The people have been learning that they can use their own money to their own profit, and have begun putting their money at work for themselves by organizing and financing companies to develop profitable industries in which they will get the profits, not the members of the money clique.

This movement has aroused the antagonism of the money clique, and its members have organized every form of opposition to it.

In its most virulent form this opposition has manifested itself in an owned, subsidized or "kept" press, that prattles the manifest financial falsehoods that the money clique dictates to it. One of these falsehoods is that speculation is gambling, another is that scientific investment is speculation. Therefore, they say, "scientific investment is gambling." The cunning and devilish misapplication of these two words is the direct cause of our present condition wherein the rich are becoming richer, while the poor are becoming poorer.

DISCOURSE V.

Speculation is legitimate, but it is not investment. Speculation sometimes nearly approaches gambling, while true investment never does. Speculation in its very nature is transitory, or ephemeral, while investment is permanent, enduring.

The odium that attaches to the word speculation in the financial world was seized on early in this campaign against the people as the most powerful weapon to be used. By distorting the meaning of the word, by using it to describe what it does not mean—by calling a sound and legitimate business venture a speculation or a gamble—they have succeeded in fooling many persons and scaring them from taking a part in the establishing of new enterprises.

If you intend to buy a piece of good land and develop it to raise profitable crops, the "kept" press tells you to beware—it is a "speculation".

If you intend to open a store in a community in which every sensible person will admit there is profitable trade, the "kept" press yells "speculation" at you.

If you intend to begin manufacturing and selling a patented article that every one knows will have a large and profitable sale, the "kept" press tells you not to do it because it will be a "speculation", or a "gamble".

And so it goes along the length of the industrial line. You are dinned at from every "kept" editorial room not to do anything with your money that will give you ALL your money earns. From every quarter of the Middle Age darkness of the money clique's financial night are thrown at you a multiplicity of this javelin "speculation", electrically illuminated so you can not fail to see it.

"There's a reason." By howling "speculation" when the people are considering investing —true, scientific investment—they frighten great numbers of people away from investment; at the same time through their false and often fraudulent representations that investment means lending, they succeed in inducing great numbers of people to forego the rich returns of true investment and content themselves with lending their money for mere interest, buying bonds, etc.—evidences of money loaned. In this way the borrowers thrive, while the toilers and lenders languish.

In investing, in speculating, in gambling one takes a chance with his money. In gambling his chances of success are never greater than one out of two, often one out of ten thousand, or a million. In speculation, if founded on rule or reason, his chances of success are far greater, depending only on the future rise and fall of prices. While in true investment his chances of success depend only on the natural earning power of money put actively at work in a business opportunity under honest and efficient management. Thus his chances of success in true investment are far greater than in either of the others, and no risks are run if the business opportunity is genuine and the money is used honestly and efficiently—both of which can be easily predetermined.

Let us look into this plan of action thus falsely labeled "speculation"—all true investing is called "speculation" by the "kept" press of the money ring.

We have seen that from the fact that in speculating one takes a chance with his money and that in investing he takes a chance (though a lesser one) with his money, it has grown to be a custom with the enemies of popular investment, to call all chances of money-making "speculation". In the sense that the word has thus come to be used, what does it signify? What the evil, what the good?

What is "speculation"? And here the word will be used in the sense that the "kept" press uses it.

If, in the hospital of diseased and wounded ancient fallacies, there is one commonplace more decrepit than the rest, it is this cry of "speculation".

MAKING MONEY MAKE MONEY.

The aforetime ring-tail who first perpetrated that shibboleth has gone his way this many a day, but the work of the fool killer dieth not; his nonsense survives him. There's no "hic jacet" for it.

"Speculation" is the most abused and be-mouthed word in the English language; it is the child frightener of the financial nursery. Without it the wily promoters of the Money Trust and the old pet foxes of the bond market, ambling their 4 per cent dog churn arguments, would have no recourse except the antediluvian cry of "wolf"!

The man who putters and prattles his sparrow twitterings against honest "speculation" (true investment) is not conservative by that token. He is merely dense.

The attack on enterprising and legitimate investment is not an evidence of sanity and good reason, but the very reverse. It is the proof of an illusion, a delusion and a hallucination—"three in one"! Yea, worse, IT IS THE "FORTY DROPS" OF MENTAL COCAINE IN THE ATROPHIED BICEPS OF THE ORIGINAL DOPE FIEND—FAILURE!

Uncle Sam is now putting forth his strong arm to save unfortunate drug users from the degraded and unconscionable "dope trust". Let him also curb the harpies that thrive by their attacks on the life blood of progress—"speculation"—intelligent investment.

Forgetting for the time being business and the art of money-making and looking out over this great world and its manifold activities, what part is played by speculation?

Speculation means to look into—to find a way—to blaze a path—to go forward and not backward—upward and not downward—to have confidence rather than fear—to investigate—to try out—to stop, look, listen, and then go ahead.

Longfellow words it beautifully:

"Look not mournfully into the Past, it comes not back again. Wisely improve the Present, it is thine, and go forward to meet the Future without fear and with a manly heart."

Christopher Columbus was a speculator of the first water. Thomas A. Edison has speculated his way to undying fame. Andrew Carnegie speculated when he made the first I-beams, without which no skyscraper could have been built. Harriman speculated like a madman (apparently); the Union Pacific is his monument!

Mackay, Flood, Hearst, Stanford—all speculators—dogged determination, clear vision, absolute confidence, grit and fight—hard-hitting, rugged, fearlessness. Yes, that's it—that's what they were—SPECULATORS.

MAKING MONEY MAKE MONEY.

You cannot put your demonstrative finger on a human achievement in science, law, theology, art, industry, commerce, war or peace that is not the soul, the essence and the very breath of speculation.

Speculation is not gambling.

A speculator is not a shaker of dice.

There is no more analogy between speculation and gambling than there is between bravery and bravado, between courage and the red eye.

A man who never speculated never advanced; he was led.

The man who never speculates is not cautious; he is not wary; he is not circumspect—he is a post mortem SPECTER.

To the old Romans any people beyond their borders was barbarian.

To the modern banker, ultra-conservative, any per cent beyond his interest rate on deposits (not loans) is speculative.

Speculation is the breath of business, all the cow herders to the contrary notwithstanding.

The banks themselves are built on speculation—honest ventures—legitimate undertakings—voyages of financial, industrial and commercial adventure—all of them—every one of them.

The man who marries, speculates, in the sociological sense—otherwise he would not take her "for better or for worse".

The traveler—the rider a-horseback or the walker afoot—speculates.

The buyer, the seller, the manufacturer, the jobber, the merchant, the shopkeeper, the gatekeeper, the housekeeper—all speculating, all speculators. Life itself—and faith, too—SPECULATION! THANK GOD!

"Avaunt! and quit my sight! let earth hide
thee!
Thy bones are marrowless, thy blood is cold!
Thou hast no speculation in those eyes
Which thou dost glare with".

DISCOURSE VI.

EVOLUTION OF THE BANKING SYSTEM.

Money has been described as "frozen labor". It is in effect a draft on society for value received—a voucher to opportunity. There are many ways of looking at money, and many ways of using it, and the first thing we have to learn is that money has no fixed value, or, in other words, that its power of increasing itself is reflected accurately by the initiative and intelligence of the man who owns it, limited of course by his opportunities.

In ancient days cattle were money, and a man's wealth was gauged largely by the size of his herd; "Nabel had three thousand sheep and one thousand goats, and his wealth was very great." (1 Sam. XXV:2.)

In those old times men had to be about everything they had to do. They made right at home their own garments and other things they needed. Society was not the complex thing it is today. Their wealth was represented by cattle, but there were no cattle banks, cattle bonds, etc.; although possibly there may even then have been a type of cattle bankers, who, establishing cattle pens, gave three head of cattle for every hundred head left with them for a year, thus making the transaction equivalent to our modern banking transaction which gives $3 as interest for every $100 left in banking vaults for a year.

It is hardly probable, however, that such a condition existed, as it would have been too transparent a device even for the simple patriarchs of those days who could not have been blinded to the fact that their herd of one hundred would reproduce anywhere from one-fourth to one-half its number in the course of the year, and who certainly would not have been satisfied to take three only out of an increase of twenty-five or more.

The cattle banker would have been getting rich quick far too obviously, and we can imagine a speedy riot if the thing had been attempted; because, in the relatively simple commercial transactions of those times, the device would have exposed itself as a method by which one man, or a set of men, was gaining an undue and unwarranted advantage in getting ahead of his or their fellows.

As the world advanced the transactions of society became a great deal more complex. Cattle were not a very handy form of currency, and as men began to trade with others quite a distance from them the difficulties of effecting payment, perhaps through a hostile country, became increased so gradually, as we know it, that money was invented in the form of copper, gold and silver slugs, which derived their value from their beauty, relative scarcity, and adoption for ornamental purposes.

In due course it got so that the great majority of men could not follow their money through the intricate buying and selling fabric it had to pass, and men gradually evolved who had trained themselves to do this. These men were termed bankers.

They handled large sums of money, engaged in large commercial transactions, and in some way, not very clearly perceived, became wealthy. It was known they acted honestly, giving all who dealt with them what they guaranteed to them; and it was felt that their wealth came to them through the exercise of skill and ability not possessed by the ordinary mortal; hence, they were treated with deference and respect.

By and by, this extended a little further, and the bankers, secure in the confidence of the community, were candidly asked by some of the more wealthy people how they succeeded as they did. In many instances the methods were explained to these people, who asked to be allowed to participate with the bankers in some of the profits earned, and this the bankers permitted, on the understanding that they in turn should aid the bankers with their private wealth. This naturally led to an extension of banking operations.

The great bulk of the people, however, were not given these confidences, simply because, from the banker's standpoint, it would have been of no use. The bulk of the people had very little surplus wealth, and the little they had would be of value only if it was all collected together and the matter explained to the vast number who had it. Even if it was explained it was questionable if they would understand it; so, little by little, the bankers, instead of trying to organize a vast number of ignorant people, left them to their own resources, and confined their operations to the more intelligent and wealthy class. The poorer people, seeing these place their money with the bankers, concluded naturally that that would be a good thing for them to do, as indeed in those times it was. There was not the same law and order then as there is now, and the poor man, living in wild, unprotected parts, or on the outskirts of his village, ran the risk of losing his savings to bands of predatory men who roamed the country. So, little by little, the tiny savings of this man and that were taken in and given to the banker for safe custody.

In the gradual change from cattle to gold, it was but natural that the men who wrought in that metal should first evolve into bankers. In those days men who left their money with others were CHARGED for the accommodation. It was soon discovered, however, that moneys so left were left usually for very long terms; or, in other words, it was found that if a hundred people left a hundred thousand dollars with a banker, that only a small part of the amount would be asked back in a short time, and that only as the need for it arose. These same people would, as a matter of fact, endeavor to SAVE, so that original deposits, in lieu of being lessened gradually, tended to increase, and it was very soon seen by the banker that he would always have more money in his hands than he was asked to pay back, and that this balance or surplus would tend to increase.

On the other hand, he found many people whom he knew and trusted needed additional money, and these people were prepared to pay a reasonable sum for its use under conditions which they demonstrated to the banker would insure its repayment within a certain period.

So, between money offered and money wanted, the problem gave its own solution. The banker found his average of money drawn and money deposited, and with these figures he found that he could lend 75 per cent of what he was entrusted with, keeping 25 per cent on hand to meet current demands. As the demand for money increased he found it desirable to stimulate the depositing of money with him, and instead of charging for taking care of it he began paying for the use of it. Thus the savings interest system arose, and the discount system arose, the banker paying a SMALL interest to those who deposited money with him, and charging a LARGE interest to those who borrowed that money of him, he reaping the difference which constituted his banking profit.

Here we see the illustration of what we started to work out. In the old days cattle were money and commercial transactions were very simple, easily followed and understood. Owners of cattle would refuse to drive a hundred into a banking pen and be given three additional for the use of the hundred a year, by a cattle banker, simply because they saw that it was a bad bargain on their side.

But when metal money came into use, and transactions of commerce assumed a necessarily more complex form, this is precisely what the people did. If, for the sake of illustration merely, we assume a dollar to be equivalent to the price of a goat or a sheep, we see in these modern days the phenomenon of a hundred cattle (a hundred dollars) driven to a cattle pen (a bank), left to breed prolifically (in interest earnings) and the banker taking the balance, which may range from one-eighth to one-half or more.

The people have simply been blinded to basic facts, vitally affecting their welfare, by subtle changes that have brought custom and habit in their train, to which, in conforming, they make themselves poor and others rich.

This will develop more clearly as we proceed.

By and by the individual banker found that he was the CUSTODIAN of the money of his small depositors and MANAGER of the money of the wealthier classes. Under the law, in one transaction and another, he found a kind of partnership relation existed, or could be interpreted, between the latter class and himself. This was inconvenient and dangerous, and in seeking a remedy for this condition the corporation or company gradually evolved, such companies, as all know, limiting the liability of all concerned to a fixed amount in the event of failure. Before this, men associated together in any business enterprise could be readily ruined by the mistake or folly of one of their number, as they were all held liable for the acts of any member associate.

So joint stock companies were formed, as termed in England, or corporations, as termed here, shares of stock being created so that a wealthy man wishing to join in the enterprises of the bank could purchase as many shares of stock as he liked, and benefit pro rata to his investment.

So we find the modern bank catering to three classes, as follows:

(1) DEPOSITORS, comprising people who want their money taken care of.

(2) SHAREHOLDERS, comprising men who have bought an interest in the bank to make profits from the use of the depositors' money.

(3) BUSINESS MEN who borrow from the bank the funds of the depositors.

It will be seen at once that the money that one set of men cannot, owing to various circumstances, use profitably, is taken by another set of men and used profitably, and that the bank acts between these two classes, taking ITS profit from both their operations.

These banking profits are frequently very large. The First National Bank of New York, for instance, recently paid $4,000,000 in dividends to its five or six hundred stockholders, this calling forth the following editorial comment from the New York Journal:

"Some savings banks, including the great Bowery Savings Bank, with a million and a half depositors of small means, have cut down the rate of interest paid depositors from 4 per cent to 3½ per cent.

"Another bank, the First National, handed out a special dividend of 8 per cent, to those who own its capital stock of ten millions, and this 8 per cent was added to other dividends for the year of 32 per cent, making 40 per cent for the year.

"Quite a difference, isn't there, between putting your money as a depositor or customer in a big savings bank and intelligently putting your money as an investor in the national bank stock THAT GETS THE PROFIT?"

The two pieces of news about the special dividend for one lot of bank investors and the reduction of the rate of interest for a much bigger lot of depositors appeared, one above the other, on the front page of the conservative Evening Post. There is something in those news items to make little men think and big men chuckle:

"The gentlemen who tell you that they must cut down the rate of interest on your little savings from 4 per cent to 3½ per cent explain to you that times are VERY hard, indeed, in the banking business. And they can't pay you more. * * * The American system is pretty well illustrated in these separate items of bank news. The story of the First National Bank is a pretty fairy story for the intelligent men who buy bank stocks instead of putting their money into savings bank books.

"This year every man who had one hundred dollars invested in the First National Bank got FORTY dollars back as interest on his hundred.

"Quite a contrast between this and the three dollars and a half that the little savings bank man is to get on HIS hundred.

"Once this First National Bank did business in a quiet way on a capital of five hundred thousand dollars.

"It paid then 100 PER CENT A YEAR. Every man who had a dollar in (the shares of) the bank got a dollar every year. Rather nice for the stockholders.

"Then the capital was increased to ten millions, seven years ago. On this amount they paid 20 per cent, or two million dollars in dividends each year, until three years ago; then they paid 32 per cent, and now they pay 40 per cent.

DISCOURSE VI.

"In other words, the men that have ten millions invested in that stock get FOUR MILLIONS OF DOLLARS IN YEARLY INTEREST.

"And do not forget that this little 40 per cent looks rather small compared to something that once happened to those stockholders.

"In 1902, when the capital was increased from five hundred thousand to ten millions of dollars, they gave to every stockholder NINETEEN HUNDRED PER CENT ON HIS INVESTMENT.

"In other words, they gave the people who were intelligent enough to 'GET IN ON THE INSIDE' nineteen dollars for every dollar invested. They handed them ten millions of dollars in exchange for half a million. And now they pay them 40 per cent on that ten million. Half a million changed into ten millions and 40 per cent a year interest on the ten millions—very nice, indeed."

Such a contrast, as the Journal very pertinently remarks, should cause "the little man" to do some thinking and studying to make that little brain of his better if he can.

This isolated instance taken from among many may well cause us to pause and reflect if something is not wrong with our civilized methods and habits—a something the more uncivilized man would not commit, because in the simpler state of society in which he lived he would have seen his error very soon.

When we pause to reflect and analyze we see that about 5 per cent of society are living in wealth and independence, and the remaining 95 per cent are living in a very different condition.

Very few people die in possession of a competency. Yet, if wealth was more evenly distributed, all should. This condition has come about in a very subtle way. Basically it has not been the result of a conspiracy of brains, but simply a difference in brains. While one class has profited at the expense of the other, it has not basically striven to do this. It has simply taken what lay at its hands. Bankers are honorable men, and they cannot be blamed for studying their own interests. They are money-makers, not reformers, and they realize they cannot, individually, reform the world. They accept and use conditions as they find them.

The remedy, undoubtedly, lies in a wider financial education of the masses, as against the classes who see to it that they achieve it anyhow.

There is a way out, and a very simple way. The people have simply to learn the difference between the RENTAL of money, the limited earning power of money, and the FULL EARNING POWER of money.

We see a little fruit huckster take his hand cart, invest $10 in a stock of fruit and make 25 per cent or more on his DAILY investment. Each day he is given an object lesson on what money REALLY earns. He sees that if he can extend his operations he can increase his profits, and he sees also that if he hopes to increase his profits he must have a larger capital.

So he begins to SAVE. Realizing the risk he runs if he hoards his money, he takes it to a great bank and deposits it. When he wants it back he can get it. He thinks in a small way and in a narrow circle, however, and becomes a SAVER in lieu of a MAKER. What he HAS is a certainty. What he MAY HAVE as a result of what he has, is an uncertainty. So he rests satisfied with his "nest egg", and his pleasure and ambition to see it growing steadily year by year. Actually he has RENTED his money at a NOMINAL rental to people who, unlike himself, see clearly what they MAY HAVE from what they can get.

So they pass him in the race for fortune. They have not oppressed him, or even taken advantage of him. He is simply a victim to his own habits of thought. It is not the particular business of the bank to educate him, nor of anyone connected with the bank. So Tony goes back to Italy after a while with a little fortune of a thousand dollars or so, earned by years of hardship and toil, while others have taken the money he amassed, as he amassed it, and by its meantime USE have made ten times a thousand to the one Tony made.

He was ignorant, had suffered by his ignorance, but withall, was entirely satisfied. From such material come the fortunes of the upper class. FROM SUCH CONDITIONS WE MUST PERCEIVE AND DRAW CORRECT DEDUCTIONS unless we, like Tony, are satisfied with things as they are. In that event we may rest assured that keener wits are capitalizing our inertia and forging ahead on the fruit of our labor and toil.

As the coster said: "You pays your money and you takes your choice". To get ahead, get a head.

Now, if Tony had put his thousand dollars into National Bank Stock at the right time, we have seen that it would have grown to nineteen thousand dollars, besides paying him as much as a thousand dollars a year additional while growing. IF he had. But as we proceed we will learn that men like Tony are not permitted to put their thousand in and take nineteen thousand out. He is not forcibly barred from doing so, but he is pretty effectively headed off all the same; and if, defeated in banking channels, he seeks to duplicate that opportunity in the thousand and one channels open to him in this broad land of America, "another name for opportunity", we will see he is rendered so timid and frightened that he will never do it. So he is subtly led to continue his little contribution to the big bank cattle pen, taking a tenth of what he could get, and kept, withal, quite happy and contented.

We will, in fact, see a series of contrasts quite as startling as the 3½ per cent offered Tony by a bank, and the 40 per cent given to the shareholders of a bank, and we will appreciate the bewilderment of poor Tony better as we proceed when he is solemnly warned by one publication that his money cannot be safe if it earns much more than 4 per cent, and reads in the next issue of his morning paper that the Fifth Avenue Bank has paid a dividend of 230 per cent, and but for his reverence for all that appertains to banks and banking, he would assuredly wonder if that bank was safe, because evidently his simple mind might assume that it necessarily followed that its shareholders must be engaged in a highly reckless enterprise!

But if he assumed, as he doubtless would, that bankers move in a higher world than he, his faith in the adjuration to rest content with 4 per cent, or so, might receive a shock when he found Wells Fargo declaring a 300 per cent dividend, the American Tobacco Company declaring a 40 per cent dividend, and the Pullman Company gathering profits of over $33,000,000 on an original capital of $1,250,000.

If of a questioning disposition, he might ask someone who knew if these concerns are sound and stable, and on being assured that they are, and finding that hundreds of concerns with similar earning power are sound and stable, he might, in his simplicity, class the editor as a LIAR, or WORSE.

As a matter of fact, Tony has to learn that there are many exceptions to the investment rule—so many, in fact, that it is no rule at all—only a claimed rule, fitted for the consumption of Tony and his class, their aggregate savings being VERY useful.

Assuming that he lived here about 1887, he might have deposited $100 in his bank and then become curious enough to follow it through his bank into the hands of a borrower from that bank, and he could have seen that hundred dollars purchase shares of stock that a little later became worth thirty thousand dollars or more. Had he done this, it is safe to say Tony would never have gone back to Italy.

DISCOURSE VI.

"It is true", writes Mrs. Chase in a letter to the editor of Business and Finance, "that twenty years ago I bought shares of United Verde stock for $100—also that I refused $35,000 for it".

Tony might have learned that money is simply a voucher to opportunity, and that the power of increasing itself is reflected accurately by the initiative and intelligence of the man who owns it.

DISCOURSE VII.

THE BLINDING FABRIC OF FINANCE.

After reading the previous article explaining the perplexity of Tony who is told by prominent magazines, presumably issued for his guidance, that any investment offering him more than 4 or 5 per cent is unsafe, or worse, and then have seen Tony pick up current newspapers and find one of the biggest and soundest banks in the country paying 40 per cent, and great industrial and commercial concerns paying very much more, you will well appreciate his bewilderment, and will excuse him for writing in his own lame English to one of the great magazines asking if Wells Fargo, American Tobacco Company, or the Pullman Company are "get-rich-quick" concerns, as they are paying far greater sums than he is told any sound concern can pay.

We can imagine the dignified editor of such a great magazine placed on the horns of a dilemma, and we can be excused for a little curiosity as to the precise way in which he would answer Tony's simple inquiry.

He might be inclined to tell Tony that he could not get the same earnings on his money, simply because he was too ignorant and lacked the power of judgment and discrimination that other men possess; but he would hardly be inclined to be so plain with Tony and his class, because it might then occur to Tony that if education was the key to such successes, he had better get education. In the absence of a satisfactory explanation he might proceed to get it anyhow, and he would be wise if he did.

Tony would begin to read and study, and, as he progressed, he would find certain facts that would shatter his belief in the whole investment creed that he had been asked to believe religiously. He would find that the high priests of finance were, if not misleading him, at least preying on his ignorance, precisely as the "medicine man" preys on the igorance of the tribe, or as tribes of old were ruled with an iron hand by graven images unapproachable by the laity, which, when angry, belched fire from their mouths, and made strange and terrifying sounds that portended disaster and death to those who were inclined to depart from the orthodox beliefs through which the shrewder brains ruled the tribe.

As Tony progressed in enlightenment, and found the blessings that intelligence and education confer, he would discover that the strings and levers of the financial god were being pulled and manipulated by the votaries of the financial religion with the express object of keeping him and his class in the poverty and servitude that they consider necessary to their own ends.

He would, as he progressed, dare to lift his head, as the terrifying ritual progressed, and ask whether the men who stood above him on the sacrificial altar moved in a higher world, or simply claimed they did. As he watched he would view the machinery of manipulation and realize that he and his fellows were dupes.

And, as he watched, he would find others thinking as he felt, and seeing what he saw. Renouncing his erstwhile faith that had bound him in superstitious chains, he would depart for another country, there to find prophets of a new day who would show and teach him that all men were born with equal opportunities, and that the man of brains and discrimination need not lean on the iron clad tenets of a financial creed that taught him that a little independence by SAVING was all he could hope for.

He would find great and good men appealing to his REASON rather than to his FEAR, telling him in the words of a famous judge:

"I should like to see well managed industrial corporations popularized through the ownership of their securities by great numbers of people with small means, so that savings banks will decline in popularity and their deposits dwindle''.

He would find that good and educated men, like Professor Edward Sherwood Meade, were saying:

''The actual earnings of a sum of money expended in some form of production were never greater than now. While the investment rate of interest has steadily fallen, the productivity of funds, contributed by the investor, has steadily advanced. For the last four years, for example, to the personal knowledge of the writer, the annual earnings of certain well equipped steel plants have approximated 100 per cent on their cost. The majority of well-managed manufacturing establishments and mining plants have made more money than they care to confess. The profits on successful enterprises are far greater than the return on good securities. There is no reason to doubt that these profits will continue to increase.''

If Tony, whose mentality is now thoroughly awake, decides to push his investigation further and find what is meant by ''securities'', he will find that ''securities'', in the parlance of bankers, consist of BONDS, and that a BOND is a form of instrument that takes a thousand dollars from him, and, after retaining it for thirty or fifty years, gives it back to him. He will also find that under the terms of this bond he is paid from 4 per cent to 5 per cent on his money, or, in other words he will get $4 or $5 each year for each $100 he lends. He will also find that this bond is, as a rule, perfectly SAFE, as that word is understood in investments, because property worth double its value, or more, is pledged to him and other bondholders to secure it.

Yes, Tony's money will, in most instances, be SAFE. He will find the high priests of finance scrupulously honest gentlemen who will do exactly as they agree to do, and, if the income suits him, his life will be as happy and as comfortable as each member of the barbarian tribe who scrupulously observed the tenets taught him by the claimed servant of the brazen image he worshiped, who periodically appeared before the rude, lean and hungry tribe in gorgeous robes of splendid texture, fat and sleek as a man should be who was the earthly instrument of a greater power.

But if Tony examined this transaction a little further he would find that a set of men called stockholders got the money of the bondholders, and, setting it to work in some PRODUCTIVE FORM OF INDUSTRY, made dollars to the bondholders' cents, precisely as the depositor of $100 got $3.50 a year from the savings bank, while the SHAREHOLDERS of the First National Bank got $100 a year for each $100 they had invested.

And if Tony had read the article that preceded this, he would begin to wonder if this system was not precisely the same as if, possessing 100 head of cattle, he loaned that 100 head to a large cattle owner, who would, by natural annual increase, take 25 new calves each year, and give him three or four calves only.

Tony would see a very precise and exact analogy between the two transactions, and in the strength of his newly found education, he would begin to ask himself why he took a small part of the whole when he could have the whole.

And he might ask WHY the magazine editors assiduously told him that he should buy 4 and 5 per cent bonds. And, by this time, having developed powers of observation, he might see that these same editors had to make money, and that bond dealers and bankers were helping them to make money by buying their expensive advertising space to advertise their bonds, and that, to encourage them to buy more space, and thus make them more money, the editors were using their power and influence, as highly respected and influential publishers, to convince their readers that when they bought investments, bonds were the things for them to buy, and nothing else.

Considerable light might be dawning on Tony's mind. If he had that pertinacious and troublesome kind of disposition that persists in looking for TRUTH, he might begin to suspect that these journalistic priests were pulling and manipulating the levers of the financial god he was asked to worship, simply for their own aggrandizement, and seeking to terrorize him with the fear of poverty and loss if he dared question their wisdom and infallibility.

Still they might deign to argue with him—to quiet or repress the spirit of rebellion that was evidently arising; for Tony alone they might have little respect, but for the millions of his fellows they have a good deal of respect—the respect of the minority against the power of the majority. IF TONY SHOULD SPREAD HIS "HERESIES", WOULD NOT THE WHOLE FABRIC OF MINORITY POWER AND PRESTIGE TOTTER AND FALL?

So he would be cited instance after instance of great commercial concerns paying but 4 or 5 per cent EVEN TO THEIR STOCKHOLDERS. These abnormal earnings of SOME concerns, he would be told, were EXCEPTIONS—phenomena as remarkable and as rare as eclipses of the sun or moon in old tribal experiences.

As he pondered and rebuked himself for his lack of faith he might pick up a publication whose province was to give NEWS in lieu of "information" or "education", and he might read this in the New York Times:

"Disclosing the fact that the First National Bank of New York had made profits of $86,504,091 in the less than 50 years since its organization with $500,000 capital, George F. Baker, chairman of the board of directors of that institution and its former president, gave some impressive testimony today before the Pujo 'Money Trust' Committee.

"During its existence the bank has declared dividends, he showed, of $50,850,000. Its capital was raised in 1901 to $10,000,000 by the declaration of a 1,900 per cent dividend on the original capital, while in 1908 it earned net profits of $10,677,092 and declared $12,600,000 dividends in that year, when the First Security Company was organized. During the four years between 1908 and 1911, inclusive, the dividends of the bank aggregated 226 per cent".

Tony's elemental mind by this time has come to a sharper and cleaner focus, and several items in this bit of news cause him to THINK.

He has learned that a bank keeps the money

of other people for them. He has learned that it also USES that money—that the money by no means stays in its vaults. He has learned that business men come to the bank and borrow the money that he and others have put in it. He has learned that these business men make money on the money they borrow. It is pretty easy for Tony to conclude that if the bank MAKES these great sums of money, the business men who USE the funds of the bank must make MORE money; consequently, great though the earnings of the bank may be, the EARNINGS OF INDUSTRY MUST BE GREATER, and he begins to think that, if he cannot get a share of the profits of the bank, he perhaps can get a share of the profits of industry.

You see Tony is really working back to his business beginning where he invested $10 in a stock of fruit and made 25 per cent on his DAILY investment. He is beginning to realize that the money which in his hands made more money can still continue to make more money when it passes into the hands of third parties, provided those third parties RENDER HIM A TRUE AND FAITHFUL ACCOUNTING OF ITS FULL EARNINGS.

He begins to realize that a contract, faithfully and conscientiously carried out, to pay him five dollars a year for each one hundred dollars he gives up is a very unfavorable contract to him, and that in making it he has simply suffered from his own ignorance.

Tony is learning fast.

But there is another item in this bit of news that rivets Tony's attention as an elemental but coming man of business.

He asks: "WHY, if this bank had so much money on hand, DOES IT INCREASE ITS CAPITAL?"

He is finding out many interesting things by asking himself simple questions and then seeking their answers; so he begins to follow this out and see where it leads to. He goes into the mazes of corporation creation, and he finds first that capitalization is not necessarily MONEY. He finds capital may be represented by pieces of paper called shares of stock, and he finds that dividends are sometimes payable in those shares of stock. He finds this interesting little item in one of his papers that give NEWS—that are dealing with the REALITIES of life:

"The Pullman Company started nearly fifty years ago with a capital of $1,250,000. It has never had any new capital paid in, but STOCK DIVIDENDS have increased its capital until it is now $120,000,000."

DISCOURSE VII.

And Tony reasons something like this:

"Suppose I form a little fruit company with a capital of $1,000, and suppose that company earns in the first year $1,000, and suppose I do not want people to know it is earning so much, what will I do? It seems to me that I could increase its capital stock to $20,000, divide this additional $19,000 shares of stock among the people who held the original thousand, then take the cash profits for the year of $1,000 and pay these people who, holding all the shares of stock, would get just the same amount as under the original arrangement.

"By this process", reasons Tony, "the company, instead of declaring a dividend of 100 per cent on its original capital of $1,000, would be declaring a dividend of 5 per cent on its capital of $20,000.

"If this was done quietly and privately, the company, so far as the outside public was concerned, would be earning only 5 per cent. It would be announced in the papers that my fruit company had paid a 5 per cent dividend. That would certainly deceive people as to its true earnings.

"Furthermore, it would sound very CONSERVATIVE."

Tony has seen a great light. He is becoming a veritable high priest himself.

From this on Tony progresses very rapidly. His education is no longer theoretical, but intensely practical. He puts his ideas into force, forms his little company, and in due course increases its capitalization from $1,000 to $20,000, and finds his interest therein grown nineteen times greater.

In other words, he has nineteen shares more than the one he originally had; and the shares are paying 5 per cent; and the great magazines are exhorting their readers to buy nothing promising over 5 per cent, as it is unsafe; and the readers of those great magazines are faithfully heeding the exhortations of their financial high priests; and Tony has nineteen shares in his possession where before he had one, representing, say, an original investment in cash of $10; and, right in his hands is the chance of selling those nineteen shares at $10 each for $190 to the followers of those priestly editors.

This is all somewhat bewildering to Tony. It looks unreal, but the hard cash is a very real thing. Following his original strain of doggedness, he finds that almost unconsciously he has penetrated to the innermost temple of financial worship and is a high priest himself, chanting the vesper creed of "5 per cent and safety."

Outside Tony's company, the unorthodox worshipers chant the newer, truer and more ennobling creed of "get what your money earns" to the ears of the enslaved multitude who take no heed. "Fools", cries Tony. "They would tell these people more than is good for them to know. I have earned my right to this extra money, because I have used my brains. The cattle they strive to teach have not. They are dense, stupid, ignorant—tools for men of finer mind and fibre like me." And he reads with satisfaction the item that the Pullman Company paid eight per cent dividends on its capital of $120,000,000, with the mental note that it is too high, slightly beyond the orthodox yield, and that he, with others, will exert their influence to cause the guiding lights of that company to increase the capital until the dividend rate falls to the orthodox proportion of 5 per cent again.

So Tony ranks himself with class in lieu of mass. Thereafter he is a thoroughgoing conservative. As he progresses, he joins the directorate of most "conservative" banking institutions, reads the most "conservative" magazines, associates with the most "conservative" financial people and bitterly condemns the "yellow sheets" that, by injudicious editorials, disclose the mechanism through which the high priests of the sacred temple of finance accomplish their wonders and move "in a higher sphere."

And, withal, he finds justification. "The people are ignorant", he cries. "They will be imposed on by imitations of real opportunities. They cannot judge. They cannot discriminate. Better by far that I take nineteen parts of what their money earns and give them one-twentieth of it, than that they should lose that twentieth. That money makes me rich and powerful, and my wealth will be used for the public good. I will endow libraries, found hospitals, liberally contribute to charity. The people will be better for my rule."

But he is wrong. He knows it, otherwise why this elaborate fabric of financial deceit? He takes the herd (dollars) of the poor shepherd and deliberately deceives him in regard to its productive capacity—takes the fruit of his toil and labor—imposes on his ignorance and lack of knowledge by blinding him with the intricacies of the modern commercial and financial structure. It is inherently unjust, and injustice cannot live.

So we find the newer ideal—the corporation formed by common people, capitalized to produce the sum of money necessary for the operations it contemplates, and formed under conditions by which the people are given an opportunity to subscribe for its ORIGINAL issue of capital stock, and that they will get ALL the profit it earns, whatever that profit may be; and the shares of stock of this corporation will be offered and tendered to the common people, and not to any financial "clique", be its name capitalists, bankers or underwriters.

Between that and the corporation-baby fostered by Tony and his class, there is a distinction as wide as the poles. Tony and his class realize its menace to them and seek to discredit or kill it, pausing at nothing to accomplish their ends. But they will fail. The law of progress is against them, and the people, with the spread of education and enlightenment, are coming into their own, and we will see:

"Well managed corporations, popularized through the ownership of their securities by great numbers of people, so that savings banks will decline in popularity and their deposits dwindle."

And now, where and how?

For answer let us take Emerson's inspirational statement as our keynote:

"America! Another name for Opportunity. Our whole history reads like a last effort of the Divine Providence on behalf of the whole human race."

DISCOURSE VIII.

AMERICA! ANOTHER NAME FOR OPPORTUNITY.

We find in every community an old-timer who can remember when he could have got the lot on which the courthouse now stands "for a song", or bought all the business district for a few cows or horses. He looks back, sees his mistake, and regrets his loss.

But won't his son, when he reaches his age, have a similar plaint to make? The writer remembers that in his youth he hunted over a section of country that is now a populous town. We see clearly enough the link between past and present, but what befogs us is the link between present and future. There were great opportunities in America in the time of the Astors and the Vanderbilts, but there are greater opportunities now.

There is only one way of judging the future, and that is by a review of the history of the past. The population of Germany is nearly equal to that of the United States, yet the empire of Germany is about the size of the state of Texas. Consider a fact like that, and you will at once see that even today the United States is very thinly populated, and that, in the natural progress of the world, a greater and greater population must pour in, and, as more come, they create increased wealth and increased opportunities.

Review these figures of the growth of the United States very carefully:

1800	5,308,483
1850	23,191,876
1880	50,155,783
1900	75,994,575
1910	92,174,515
1914 (estimated)	98,646,491

Now note how population has created WEALTH:

1850	$ 7,135,780,000
1880	42,642,000,000
1900	88,517,306,775
1910	107,104,211,917

Now note how the wealth per capita has kept pace with the general increase:

1850	$ 307.59
1880	850.20
1900	1,164.79
1910	1,310.11

It will be seen from these fundamental figures that as population increased, wealth increased, that the average wealth for each person became greater and greater. This condition is likely to continue for centuries, as we find the following inflow of population each year:

1908	782,870
1909	751,786
1910	1,041,570
1911	878,587
1912	838,172
1913	1,197,892
1914	1,218,480

These are recent figures. Traced further back they carry their own moral. The total number of immigrants since 1820, for instance, is 32,027,424.

Wherever we examine statistical records we find the ratio of increasing wealth corresponding to population, as clearly seen in our manufacture, our banks, our fisheries, our farms and our mines. The value of manufactured products, for instance, produced in 1850, was $1,019,106,616, and in 1910 their value had risen to $20,672,051,870, while deposits in savings banks increased from about forty-three and a half million dollars in 1850 to over four and a half BILLIONS in 1914.

"In the basic elements of economic progress", states the Department of Commerce, "the United States ranks high among the nations of the world, being one of only five countries having an area in excess of three million square miles, and the only nation of the western world (except Russia) having a population of over 100,000,000. In the interchange of products among its own people it leads the world, its home trade at the present time being estimated at nearly forty billion dollars, or equal to the international exchange of the world and approximately ten times the value of our foreign trade, now valued at four billion dollars.

"That our present foreign trade is far short of its immediate possibilities is evident from a consideration of its area, commerce, and other economic factors in comparison with that of other leading countries; thus the present export trade of the United States (two and a half billion dollars) represents about $25 per capita. A per capita basis equal to that of Argentina would raise the exports of the United States to five billion dollars, and one equal to that of Belgium would bring its exports to ten billion dollars a year.

"Temporary recessions have frequently marked the course of American commerce, but the tendency, according to historical tables published in the 'Statistical Abstract', is ever higher. In eleven years, from 1890 to 1901, our foreign trade grew from one and a half billion to two and a fourth billion dollars, an increase of 50 per cent, while in the eleven years from 1902 to 1913 it increased from two and a fourth to four and a fourth billions, a gain of 90 per cent.

"The foundations of this growth are laid deep in the soil and natural resources of our country, and in the character of our people. Thus, the American Union, from 13 states having 325 thousand square miles and one million people, has expanded to 48 states and the territories of Alaska, Porto Rico and Hawaii, with an area of three and two-thirds million square miles and one hundred million people. In the period since 1870 the value of our farm products has risen from two billion to about ten billion dollars a year; the output of coal from less than thirty to nearly five hundred million long tons; pig iron from two to thirty-one million tons; petroleum from two hundred twenty-one million to nine and a fourth billion gallons; and manufactures from four billion to over twenty billion dollars."

These are hard statistical facts, yet what fairy-like actualities they demonstrate—the making of a great nation—the making of great individual wealth proceeding constantly, uniformly, systematically, yearly, monthly, weekly, daily. The tremendous wheel of progress going round, bringing prizes of wealth and realized ambition to all who grasp them as they pass—a daily story of men flung on golden thrones by the onrushing tide of opportunity—a tale of men poor yesterday and rich today—a spectacular record of dimes turned to dollars, and dollars into hundreds of thousands of dollars in incredibly brief periods—the modest beginnings of young corporations and their marvelous climb to great business enterprises, sustaining and enriching thousands who have joined them. Let us examine the records of trade and commerce and see if the INDIVIDUAL gets his fair share of opportunity in this stupendous rolling up of national wealth.

For years the patent office declined to consider any flying machine applications, taking the ground that the navigation of the air by a heavier-than-air machine was impossible. But a few men hung to the IDEA, even in the face of this damning verdict from what may be justly considered the highest technical authority in the country. The shareholders of the companies manufacturing flying machines and accessories are now reaping a rich reward for their defiance of traditional conservatism.

In the year of "depression", 1914, the United Cigar Stores of New Jersey made a dividend distribution of 110 per cent, and Woolworth, selling the commonest and cheapest of articles, made total sales of $66,228,072, which exceeded the gross earnings of the Erie Railroad, and beat the great Adams Express Company in volume of business nearly 50 per cent. The Farmers and Mechanics Bank of Sharpsburg declared a dividend of 100 per cent, and the stockholders of the Fidelity Trust Company divided a "melon" of $7,000,000. The First National Bank of Uniontown declared a dividend of 700 per cent, and another $10,000,000 "melon" was cut by the Vacuum Oil Company. The Ford Motor Company made about $25,000,000 profits on a capitalization of $2,000,000, and the mere "good-will" of Cluett, Peabody & Company, manufacturing such prosaic articles as shirts and collars, formed a very large part of the $18,000,000 corporation into which it was recently formed. The mere "good-will" of Sears, Roebuck & Company was valued at $30,000,000, or 75 per cent of its common stock issue. The "good-will" of the Woolworth Company was valued at $50,000,000, and of the B. F. Goodrich Company at $57,000,000. In these few isolated cases (and hundreds could be quoted almost at random) we see the progress of the United States reflected in its business units, and we see the wonderful opportunity for aggrandizement that these business units offer to those who purchased stock in them in the earlier stages of their development.

Continuous payments of such dividends means that the par value of the shares of stock on which such dividends are paid INCREASES TWENTY TIMES IN VALUES, so that a share of stock with a par value of $100 would sell under such conditions, for $2,000, because, under present conditions, a stock earning 5 per cent continuously sells at par, and if it earns 10 per cent, double par; and so on.

Shares of stock of the Astor National Bank, for instance, which paid 25 per cent dividend, sold at $605 a share, and stock of the Central Trust Company, which paid 45 per cent in 1910, sold at $1,030 a share, though the par value was $100. The $100 shares of stock of the Union Trust Company, which paid 60 per cent, had a ready market at $2,500 a share.

It is customary for many companies, however, to pay their dividends IN NEW SHARES OF STOCK for the purpose of concealing their real earnings. Suppose a corporation is capitalized for $100,000, and it earns $10,000, or 10 per cent on its capitalization. That company could increase its capital stock $100,000 more, and give this to its shareholders in lieu of the cash. The next dividend would be paid on

$200,000 capitalization, thus lowering, APPARENTLY, the earnings of the corporation.

Sears, Roebuck & Company recently paid a $20,000,000 dividend to holders of the common stock. The distribution was made in new common shares, against an accumulated surplus, "a large part of which", comments the current press, "has been reinvested in the business."

It will, of course, be evident to the reader that when the shares of stock are increased, and dividends paid in stock, the next cash dividend will be divided among THE SAME NUMBER OF PERSONS, even though the shares of stock have been increased; and it will also be evident that the dividend, having to be distributed among A LARGER NUMBER OF SHARES, will be much lower, although, if the original persons hold the increased shares, their profit will be no lower.

As a matter of fact, these new shares are almost exclusively tendered TO OLD SHAREHOLDERS. Also, as a matter of fact, when they constitute a stock dividend the old shareholders are ENTITLED to them by virtue of that dividend. We thus see that when a company starts to make money the money it makes is conserved among the original shareholders, and outsiders have no chance to get in unless they pay a heavy premium for the pivilege;

and we again see that the way to make money is to get into new companies when they are offering the first authorized capitalization for investment subscription.

And there you have a big part of the secret of money making—GET INTO THE COMPANY WHILE IT IS YOUNG. If you do not do this, you will usually be buying, at par or more, additional shares of stock that have been issued as stock dividends to old shareholders.

If a company originally had a capitalization of $100,000, and that had been increased to $1,000,000, and the $900,000 IN SHARES OF STOCK thus created had been distributed among the original purchasers of the first $100,000 in shares of stock offered, you will see that, assuming the par value was $100 a share, original investors purchased 1,000 shares and were GIVEN later, as capitalization increased, 9,000 additional shares. In other words, each man who originally bought and paid for ONE share would have NINE MORE SHARES for which he had not paid, but which he received as profits, while the money these shares represented remains in the business, of which he is part owner, to earn him more profits.

Stop at that paragraph and be sure you understand it thoroughly before you read further—THOROUGHLY.

Now, if that corporation is earning and paying 5 per cent on its one million dollars of capitalization, the shares of stock are worth "par", or $100 a share in the open market; and that is what you will have to pay for them if you want to get into that corporation.

The man who bought ONE share when that company was organized, and who since received nine more, may be glad to retain the original share for which he paid $100, and sell you the nine additional he has for $900. It may look like a big price to pay when you know all the circumstances, but you must remember that this is his reward for COURAGE AND JUDGMENT.

He put up $100 of his hard earned money before that corporation began to pay dividends, and perhaps before it had even started to do business.

In a sense he took a risk, and in another sense he took no risk. In other words, he brought his business training to judge of the probabilities or otherwise of the success of that company.

His JUDGMENT told him that the company had a good product or a good proposition. Then COURAGE backed his opinion, and his money went into it. He won, and the directors of the company rightfully consider he should be HANDSOMELY rewarded, because where this one man did invest, and helped the company when it needed it, there were hundreds who would not invest and would not help the company when it needed it.

The directors rightfully figure that the man who had the pluck and business judgment to do what hundreds refused to do, was a good man to cultivate and take care of, and they took care of him as the illustration shows; and that is precisely what thousands of directors of old and successful companies are doing in America today.

Such companies are making profits for their insiders, but to the outsiders there is no profit —merely a LIMITED dividend or limited interest. The insiders have the cream, and are skimming it.

If you are an "outsider" you must observe what these successful men do, and do as they do. Fortunately, in this progressive land of America, you have the opportunity. In the great aggregate increase of the annual national wealth we find new corporations taking up and developing multitudinous opportunities created by population increase, and the undeveloped resources of the country. These corporations have to START, they have to GROW, they have to EARN, and, wisely managed, THEY, TOO, enter the dividend paying stage. When they earn 5 per cent your money is returnable, as their stock can always be sold at par. When they earn 10 per cent your investment has DOUBLED in value, and if they pay 100 per cent your investment has increased twenty times in value. If, in lieu of paying a dividend in cash that the cash profits may be used in building the business bigger to earn still greater profits, they pay it to you in shares of stock, or, if in addition to paying you the cash dividend they also pay you a stock dividend to conceal the big earnings of the company, you may sell that stock to "outsiders"; and if your first share cost you $100 and you have received nine more, then you can keep the first and sell the nine for $900—or sell any part of the nine you choose, and hold the rest. Many men hold all their shares and make thousands of dollars from an original investment of perhaps a hundred dollars, and many men with but a hundred dollars in such an investment have become, through dividends paid, independent for life.

A continued application of this principle makes millionaires. It is scientific investing for profit—for large profits.

MAKING MONEY MAKE MONEY.

To make money, seek opportunities. Then invest in the original shares of well organized and honestly and competently managed companies engaged in developing and commercializing good opportunities.

DISCOURSE IX.

THE BANKS AND THE PEOPLE.

Hundreds of years ago, when people got money they carried it about their person, or, if they did not like to take that risk, they buried or hid it. In other words, money was HOARDED.

After a while certain men in every community came to be trusted. People took their money to these men and asked them to take care of it. As a rule, these men had better facilities for taking care of it, possessing strong dwelling places, large retinues of servitors, or soldiers, who protected their masters' property. Manifestly, money was safer with them than with ignorant and unprotected peasants.

In course of time these men were called "bankers", and for a long time they charged people for taking care of their money, so that when a peasant saved up a certain sum and placed it with the banker, he would, when he went to draw it out, get a smaller sum than he had deposited.

The facts were that while the peasants trusted the banker, the banker had not learned to trust the people. When the bankers learned to do this, they found that they could pay the peasants something for leaving their money with them.

That was a big forward leap, and the world took wonderful strides in commerce and industry when it was made. Sometimes, however, it takes very long periods of time before old habits are completely overcome and changed. The average man of today does not HOARD money, as used to be the universal custom, but millions are still doing what is really a very ancient and obsolete custom, namely, BANKING their money for security.

We are saved, of course, from the worst blighting effect of this world-wide habit by the fact that the bankers, in lieu of HOLDING that money in strong boxes, lend it freely to the business world. It becomes, therefore, of benefit in building up manufacture, trade and commerce.

One big economic drawback of this system, however, lies in the fact, that, while the BUSINESS world benefits from this method, the DEPOSTING world does not; and this fact prevents the far greater benefit to society and industry that would follow if the men who own the money would USE it in lieu of SAVING it.

One can readily imagine what would happen to the financial and industrial world if the bankers, overnight, made a resolution to HOLD money deposited in their vaults as the old bankers did. There would be a fearful crash in our whole economic and industrial life, and nations would be literally ruined.

But if, on the other hand, depositors, overnight, decided to USE their own money in the same fashion as the bankers now use it, there would be a most marvelous economic gain, paralleling in importance the great business revolution wrought when the old bankers found they could with safety lend their deposited money to business men.

Until the people, as a class, get from the SAVING to the MAKING habit, the whole social and industrial fabric will labor under a concealed, but nevertheless tremendously hurtful handicap.

The reason ought to be clear. Bankers form only a small percentage of the whole population. Business men, also, form but a relatively small percentage of the whole. Yet this small percentage, under present conditions, reap the TRUE earning power of money, while the infinitely larger percentage that save that money reap only a FRACTION of its earning power.

What is the consequence? Simply an unequal distribution of wealth—the contrast we all know between riches and poverty—the dominance of the few over the many—the many and varied evils with which the whole social fabric is honeycombed.

A very large proportion of the many injustices that exist is due to this UNEQUAL distribution of wealth.

If the facts are looked at squarely, and with unprejudiced eyes, this fact will be seen to be true.

Money and POWER are synonymous terms, and while the great bulk of the people continue by choice to put their entire earnings in a relatively few hands they confer POWER with the money.

And that power RULES.

And while that power rules the classes will always govern the masses.

Wealth on the whole should be distributed as uniformly as population. There will always be an inequality in wealth, and no socialistic propaganda will ever prevent it, for the very simple reason that all men are NOT equal and never will be. But while all men are not equal, that fact should not be permitted to prevent each to receive according to his ability.

Let ten men run a race—ONE will be found superior to the others. This rules in everything—even in money-making; but what we do contend is, that while all men cannot be equal, all men SHOULD BE MORE NEARLY EQUAL THAN THEY ARE AT PRESENT.

Power—which in the last analysis is money—should be more equally distributed. The favored few of the financial world are the favored few of a favored few. That may sound a little vague. What is meant is that practically five per cent of the whole population of American control the money of the remaining 95 per cent, and these five per cent are instrumental, through that reason, in making millionaires and multi-millionaires of the small percentage of their own number.

In the last analysis, a little money "clique" is advancing the members of its own clique to enormous riches.

Among themselves they control the vast fabric of commerce and industry, and, among themselves, they are wresting from the people as a whole their heritage and birthright.

Americans are dimly perceiving this. But it is of no use demolishing trusts, etc., until we alter the methods which make trusts and monopolies possible.

THE MONEY OF THE AMERICAN NATION MUST BE USED FOR THE GOOD OF THE WHOLE NATION, AND NOT, AS NOW, FOR THE GOOD OF A VERY SMALL

PERCENTAGE OF THE PEOPLE OF THE NATION.

Some men will not trust banks, but place their money in the care of the Government through the postal savings banks.

But what happens?

THE BANKS STILL GET THAT MONEY.

The Government sends it to them.

This is an exemplification of the old adage: "Of two evils choose the lesser", and money in bankers' hands is certainly better than in old teapots. But it would be infinitely better if the money was at work making its owners rich rather than creating unnecessary riches for the bankers and the clique the bankers serve, as it does now.

That is the point that every bank depositor wants to get clearly outlined in his mind.

Five per cent of the population are immensely wealthy or independently rich. The remaining 95 per cent are struggling for a living. These 95 per cent are in the position in which they are because of their financial habits, and the five per cent are in their position also because of financial habits, although of a directly opposite character.

I have just read a little paragraph that to my mind expresses the whole thing very succinctly. It reads as follows:

DISCOURSE IX.

"The difference between the man who counts his savings in hundreds and the man who builds up a fortune of thousands is that the latter uses intelligence as well as thrift."

And there's the whole lesson.

It would be a very desirable thing to reform the whole country and let all the people reap the tremendous economic benefits that would be derived.

But that may be the work of a century or more.

The better thing is to start in and reform YOURSELF.

"Charity begins at home"—and so does financial aggressiveness.

The thing NEAREST TO OUR HAND is the thing to do. And the thing nearest to our hand in this financial problem is a radical change in our INDIVIDUAL methods of handling money.

The money of each individual IS HIS OWN, and he should demand, AS HIS RIGHT, all that it will earn.

In place of LENDING TO enterprise he should become a PARTNER WITH enterprise.

No poor man can afford to LEND money at a nominal rate of interest.

What he wants to do—what he naturally feels he must do—is to MAKE money.

To make it he has to realize that dollars, put together, like everything in the world, acquire greater power, force and strength.

A single man cannot do what an army can.

A single dollar cannot do what an army of dollars can.

So he must make his dollar one of an army of dollars.

Of course he does this when he places his money in a bank, because in the stupendous wealth of the banks he has very clear evidence of the titanic power of money.

But if he puts his money in a bank, he is not a PARTNER WITH enterprise, but simply a LENDER TO enterprise.

He becomes a partner with enterprise, under precisely the right conditions, when he places his money in the treasury of a corporation which, by virtue of its articles of incorporation, is bound to divide all its profits equally among all its members in exact proportion to the size of their respective stakes in the enterprise.

He then must get what his money really earns.

Furthermore, he knows that his own dollars will join with an army of other dollars, and, by virtue of this fact, acquire greater power, force and strength.

His money, in lieu of working to pay dividends to a bank, will then be working to pay dividends to HIM.

And, in a very large sense, it is precisely like a deposit in a bank, because when the corporation begins to earn and pay dividends the shares of stock he holds acquire a market value, and if he needs the money he can always "cash in" by selling his stock in the open market.

But note this difference:

If his money was in a bank, and the bank earned and paid its shareholders 100 per cent dividends, that would not enhance the value of his deposits. If he puts $100 in, he could still draw out only $100 principal.

If, however, his money was in a corporation, and the corporation earned and paid 100 per cent dividends, his shares of stock would be worth twenty times more than he paid for them, so that if he had put in $100 he could, by selling his shares, draw out $2,000.

That's the difference between putting your money in a bank and putting it into a corporation.

There are four ways of looking at this question:

1. You can hoard money.
2. You can save money.
3. You can lend money.
4. You can MAKE money.

And when you look at the thing squarely you will see that the LAST thing is the RIGHT thing to do.

When you go into the money-making field, by becoming a PARTNER WITH industry, even if your earnings are comparatively small, they make a stupendous difference as compared with the earnings on the same amount of money loaned to industry; as, for instance, in a savings bank, at 3 per cent.

Let us illustrate this in the following way:

Smith is a man whose financial habits lead him always to deposit money in a bank at 3 per cent. He doesn't think about this much. He merely knows it's a good thing to SAVE, and he saves.

Jones is a man whose financial habits teach him to MAKE. He puts his money into industry instead of into banks, and by this different habit of thinking he gets more. But we will say he does not get MUCH more. He earns on the whole, say, 6 per cent, while Smith, of course, gets 3 per cent.

They both let principal and interest accumulate, Smith by leaving his money and interest on deposit, and Jones by reinvesting his dividends.

Well, here's the first remarkable difference that will strike you if you analyze the two cases.

Smith, the saver, will, at 3 per cent interest compounded, double his money in a trifle over TWENTY-THREE YEARS (23.278 to be exact), while Jones, the maker, will, at 6 per cent compounded by reinvestment of dividends, double his money in a trifle over ELEVEN years (11.725 to be exact).

We see quite a remarkable difference in favor of the "maker" in even this very conservative little illustration, don't we?

But, just for curiosity, let us extend that period to quite a long time and see what ultimate difference there is between the two men in fifty years. In that period, the dollar of Smith, the "saver", will have become $4.38, while the dollar of Jones, the "maker", will have become $18.42.

In other words, if both had started with $1,000, one man, SAVING, would have $4,380.

And the other man, MAKING, would have $18,420.

You may verify these figures carefully by any standard compound interest table and make SURE that they are right (they are, of course), because they show, even on that little ratio of difference, such an astounding difference between SAVING and MAKING.

And when you reflect that many corporations make 10, 15, 25 and 100 per cent, and even more, you will better understand how some men get rich so very rapidly.

And you may rest assured that MANY business corporations easily pay such dividends to their shareholders on original investments in them.

Professor Edward Sherwood Meade is an acknowledged authority on financial matters, and in his great work, "Trust Finance", he says:

"The actual earnings of a sum of money expended in some form of production were never greater than now. While the investment rate of interest has steadily fallen, the PRODUCTIVITY of the funds contributed has advanced. For the last four years, for example, to the personal knowledge of the writer, the annual earnings of certain well equipped steel plants have approximated 100 per cent on their cost. The majority of well managed manufacturing establishments and mining plants have made more money than they care to confess. These large profits are not universal, but THEY ARE NUMEROUS. There is no reason to doubt that these profits will increase."

But some persons, because of advanced age, or coming events that will require the use of their money, do not feel that they can INVEST their money; that is, put it at work permanently for LARGE PROFITS. Much of the money deposited in our savings institutions is the money of this class.

If such persons will use a little business intelligence in handling their money they need not penalize themselves by accepting the paltry 3 per cent doled out by banks, but may secure the convertibility they require and with it a doubled income. Such persons may "INVEST FOR INTEREST", which, of course, is not INVESTING, but LENDING. They should put their money into the right kind of bonds, that will mature at the time the money will be needed for other purposes.

A bond is the evidence of a LOAN. It is a written obligation to pay the principal at maturity, and interest on the same at stated intervals. In this it is like a promissory note. In addition, it is a mortgage on the government, municipality or corporation issuing it.

In buying a bond, therefore, the buyer gets such security for his money as is back of the bond, and if it is a GOOD bond he gets a definite income and his money back when the bond matures. Most bond issues are divided into sections, maturing at different times, so that one may secure bonds to mature at practically any time desired.

The important classes of bonds are Government, municipal, public utility and industrial corporation bonds, and their desirability from the viewpoint of security is in the order given.

Government bonds are not practical for the person who has but little money, because the income from them is too small.

Public utility and industrial corporation bonds are not desirable, because the security is too unstable and uncertain.

The old saying has it that nothing in this world is certain except taxes and death. Municipal bonds are, therefore, as certain as anything can be, because their interest and principal are paid by tax levy.

By selecting bonds of municipalities in our vigorous and progressive West, where money earns more than in the cramped East, and where, consequently, people can afford to pay more for its use, the bond buyer can usually get an income of 6 per cent.

Six per cent is not much for the use of money in our growing country, but it is better than 3 per cent on bank savings. And a good municipal bond is better security than the average bank.

You are simply asked to think over these facts carefully, remembering that the difference between the man who counts his savings in hundreds and the man who builds up a fortune of thousands is that the latter uses INTELLIGENCE as well as THRIFT.

You have INTELLIGENCE. These articles are giving you the KNOWLEDGE with which to USE that intelligence to the best advantage.

They constitute a mental weapon that will give you a great advantage in your personal fight for wealth and independence.

They will arm you to think along the right lines—to change your financial HABITS in a way that will redound to your personal advantage.

You have simply to look around and examine the opportunities beneath your hand to capitalize your knowledge. A very large proportion of our people do not know these things, and are INNOCENTLY suffering for that reason. There is no reason why you should suffer with them. There is no reason why YOU should remain subject to THEIR handicap.

If this and preceding articles will cause you to take an INTEREST in the NEW corporations that are constantly capitalizing opportunities for the benefit of you and other people under conditions where you MUST receive all your money earns, they will accomplish a great deal of good.

DISCOURSE X.

MASS VERSUS CLASS.

It has been pointed out that the savings of the people go into banks—that these savings are loaned by the banks (even by the Government savings banks indirectly) to financiers—that these financiers form a clique of but five per cent of our population, and that this clique, by power of the people's money, advance their favorites into positions of such tremendous power that it may be truthfully said that a very few men in America hold the nation in the hollows of their hands.

Joseph E. Davies, in a recent "System" article, stated:

"There are 305,000 corporations in the United States. Of these 296,000 have a capital, surplus and undivided profits of one million dollars or less. Only 1,600 corporations are capitalized at five million or over. But while the number of big businesses is so small, out of the 1,600 ONE HUNDRED OWN ONE-SEVENTH OF THE TOTAL PROPERTY VALUE OF THE NATION."

Now, the point is this: if these one hundred corporations should distribute widely the

EARNINGS based on the one-seventh total of the property they own, said property would in reality be held by hundreds of thousands of people, and the people as a whole would benefit.

The facts are that the EARNINGS of these corporations are being distributed to a comparatively small number of persons who hold their shares of stock. These few are being made immensely wealthy. They grow with the corporations. The corporations, on the other hand, are financing their growth by means of BONDS, or preferred NON-PROFIT SHARING stock.

In other words, in a slightly modified form we have the savings bank situation all over again. Some people, dissatisfied with the 3 per cent paid by savings banks, are buying the bonds of these corporations, which net them from 4 per cent to 5 per cent. True, they have made the difference in the earning power of their money represented by the difference in interest, but THEY ARE NOT GETTING WHAT THEIR MONEY REALLY EARNS, or anything near it. The inside "clique", holding the SHARES OF STOCK, are taking the real earnings.

Let us illustrate: American Tobacco stockholders in 1910 received dividends amounting to 40 per cent, and had received 165 per cent since organization. At that time TEN MEN owned more than 60 per cent of the stock. This company did the largest part of its financing on 4 per cent bonds and preferred stock, and in six years the company had grown so prosperous that it bought and canceled over $27,-000,000 of its bonds. It is easy to see what tremendous dividends the company will earn when its bonds are all paid off, and it is easy to see that a very small group of men will reap those earnings. It is also easy to see the difference between 4 per cent and 40 per cent, and it should be very easy to see that one group (a very large group) of men are putting up the money, while another group (a very much smaller group) are using that money and taking about all it earns.

In this case the 40 per cent dividend declared made the earnings obvious to the world, but earnings are not always so discernible because in many instances the dividends are reduced by "watering".

The masses have not a clear idea of what "watering" means, or what it effects. Let us try to get this clear, because it is very important if we are to understand all about the investment situation.

Suppose ONE MAN had a corporation capitalized for $10,000, in which he held ALL the stock, say 100 shares.

Suppose he wanted to conceal from the public any large earnings it would make.

Suppose it earned $2,000 the first year, or 20 per cent on its capitalization.

He could increase the capital stock from $10,000 to $12,000 and the company would pay its dividend in shares of stock in lieu of money.

He, of course, being the company, would receive those shares of stock.

The $2,000 profit would go into the business.

Suppose that the following year it also earned $2,000. This time that would not be 20 per cent, but less, because it would now have to be distributed over $12,000 of capitalization.

Suppose this process was repeated and repeated until the capitalization became $40,000.

At this point the annual earnings of $2,000 would be equal only to 5 per cent on the capitalization.

To the outside public the company would apparently be paying only 5 per cent dividends.

But we know that as all the shares of stock have gone to ONE MAN, that man has got NOW 400 shares in lieu of the hundred he originally had. Consequently, if the corporation at this time earns another $2,000 and pays it as a CASH dividend he gets it ALL.

DISCOURSE X.

The public reads that the corporation has earned and paid a dividend of 5 per cent on its capitalization of $40,000.

The man who owns the stock of that corporation, however, is getting 20 per cent on his original investment.

If the capital stock was increased to $80,000 by the same process the corporation would pay but a 2½ per cent dividend, and the public might regard it as a struggling business enterprise, having hard work to make both ends meet.

BUT THE INSIDE MAN WOULD BE RECEIVING 20 PER CENT ON HIS MONEY. Go over that transaction carefully if you do not fully understand it. Figure it out with pen or pencil until you DO. In view of what will follow, it is quite an important thing for you to understand.

He could also, as is most frequently done, pay himself the $2,000 as a cash dividend, and increase the capital and give himself the additional shares as a declared stock dividend. This method is commonly practiced by most corporations having many shareholders and earning exorbitant profits.

THIS "WATERING" PROCESS BLINDS THOUSANDS TO THE REAL EARNING POWER OF MONEY, and permits them to be deluded by the statement that money cannot with safety earn more than 4 or 5 per cent.

If the people are so deluded they will buy stock or bonds of corporations APPARENTLY paying but 4 or 5 per cent, in which the "insiders" are actually making 20, 40, 80, 100 or more per cent on the "outsiders" money.

Certain institutions controlled by Government, that in effect are reservoirs for the people's savings, are PROHIBITED by law from investing in anything but approved bonds.

A corporation such as we have instanced speedily arrives at a point where its bonds are approved, through the fact that for years it has paid its bond interest regularly.

The savings of the people go into these institutions, and by them are invested in these bonds.

The "insiders" are making stupendous sums of money through this financial process which seizes even the pennies of the children, and, in one vast aggregate sum annually, turns them over to the money kings who rule America.

AND THESE MONEY KINGS, AS WE HAVE SEEN, THROUGH THEIR ONE HUNDRED CORPORATIONS OWN ONE-SEVENTH OF THE PROPERTY OF THE NATION.

And their one-seventh is daily growing

larger. Each year their "grip" on national wealth and power is continuously increasing.

Subsidiary to them, and essential to them, is the whole plan of SAVING.

Subsidiary to them, and essential to them, is that portion of the press of America that persistently and insistently preaches the "saving" and "bond" creed to "thrifty", "conservative" readers.

To stigmatize the whole system as a flouting LIE is not too strong a term.

When we find an enterprise free from the tricks of the finance here explained, what do we find? Let the following from the Saturday Evening Post of February 1, 1913, answer:

"The Delaware, Lackawanna & Western is merely a railroad—not a system. It has never been reorganized, consolidated, expanded or financed. It was built from the proceeds of its capital stock and has no bonds. It traverses a rich territory and is reasonably prosperous, paying its stockholders 10 per cent a year in regular cash dividends. In 1909 it gave them, in addition, an extra cash dividend of fifty per cent, a stock dividend of fifteen per cent, and a privilege to subscribe at par to some coal stock which later sold at two hundred dollars a share and now pays ten per cent dividends. Including this privilege, the Lackawanna shareholders' melon that year amounted to about two hundred per cent—or two dollars for every dollar or par value of their stock. The next year was comparatively lean, shareholders receiving only twenty per cent cash dividends. In 1911 shareholders received, in addition to the regular ten per cent, an extra cash dividend of ten per cent and a thirty-five per cent dividend in four per cent guaranteed stock. In 1912 shareholders were given the privilege of subscribing at par to forty per cent of new stock, the right being equivalent to a dividend of one hundred and thirty-eight per cent—making altogether something like four hundred per cent in four years.

"Of course Lackawanna is quite exceptional among railroads—partly because it has been merely a railroad, rather than a dazzling subject for manipulation in Wall Street."

Again, take that statement of Henry Ford, automobile manufacturer, before the United States Industrial Relations Committee, as follows:

"How many men hold stock in your company?" Commissioner O'Connell asked.

"Only eight", replied Mr. Ford.

"What is the capitalization?"

"Two million."

DISCOURSE X.

"What was your volume of business during the last year?"

"Between $80,000,000 and $90,000,000."

"What were your profits?"

"About $25,000,000."

Here we see what money really earns when freed from the blinding veils of "watering" by recapitalization, reorganization, consolidation or expansion—we see the truth in its simple and stark but HONEST nakedness, and we find this great basic truth in every case where it has been given a chance to show itself without artificial concealment.

When the subject is studied it is found that the people as a class are getting about one-twentieth of the money their money earns, and it is found that the remaining nineteen-twentieths is going into the hands of a small "clique" of financiers, who, through the process, are gradually taking a mortgage on the great American continent. These are unassailable facts, and their significance should sink deep into every mind.

This menace has been perceived and its antidote sought in various ways. The first idea was to disintegrate those colossal combinations of capital built up through the system we have described and called "trusts". Standard Oil was attacked on this basis. November 15, 1912, the New York Times reported "oil dividends 52 per cent in dissolution year, which is four per cent more than the undissolved trust ever paid, and all profits not in yet."

Manifestly the remedy is not in that direction.

Lawson advised simultaneous withdrawal of all the people's savings from the savings banks on a certain day. As this plan was never put in force, we cannot chronicle its effects, but it would undoubtedly have been disastrous to the whole structure of commerce and credit, and would have inflicted untold hardship and misery on hundreds of thousands of perfectly innocent people. No, surcease does not lie in THAT direction.

THE REMEDY LIES EXACTLY AND PRECISELY IN A PUBLIC EDUCATION, EXPOSING THE FALLACIES THAT HONEYCOMB THE WHOLE FINANCIAL STRUCTURE, TO THE END THAT THE PEOPLE AS A WHOLE WILL DISPOSE OF THEIR SAVINGS IN SUCH FORM THAT THEY, AS A WHOLE, WILL REAP THE FULL EARNING POWER OF THOSE SAVINGS AND NOT HAND THEM OVER, AS HITHERTO, TO A SMALL FINANCIAL CLIQUE.

DISCOURSE X.

Under such a plan, bonds and preferred stock issues with limited dividends will automatically abolish themselves, and those entering the investment market will buy common stock, giving common distribution of all earnings to all shareholders in exact proportion to the amount invested.

If preferred stock is issued and bought, it will be under conditions where it is preferred as to first dividend only, and thereafter shares EQUALLY with common stock in all surplus earnings.

In other words, whatever form the financial structure takes, it will be such that all the money it earns will come back to all the people interested in it, and who render those earnings possible.

That is very simple, yet it would have the tremendous effect of diffusing wealth among the mass in lieu of a class, and it would work a tremendous revolution in the lives of everyone.

No law would be required to bring this about—people would simply refuse to invest under any other conditions, and old conditions and old structures would become obsolete for lack of financial support.

Every condition required for this revolutionary change is here now—in the hands of the people. The one lack is education—knowledge—UNDERSTANDING.

Consider these facts:

The First National Bank paid 40 per cent to its shareholders—earned from the money of its DEPOSITORS.

Depositors got 3 per cent.

American Tobacco stockholders were paid 40 per cent.

American Tobacco bondholders were paid 4 per cent.

Why do people DEPOSIT money?

Why do people buy BONDS?

Because they consider, perhaps, that shares of stock are unsafe. But are shares of stock of the First National Bank unsafe? Are those of the American Tobacco Company unsafe?

If the stock of the First National Bank is not safe, money deposited in the bank cannot be safe. A building is not stronger than its foundation.

If stock of the American Tobacco Company, representing title to all of the company's property, is not safe, its bond, being merely a mortgage on that property, is not safe.

Face these questions squarely. They are most important. Is it not apparent that the masses are led to believe that stock investments are unsafe, so that their savings will go into deposits and into bonds?

If they attempt to buy shares of stock in the "trust" corporations, are they not defeated by the system of "watering" which offers them shares that can net them but 5 or 6 per cent, when, if we get UNDERNEATH, we find the corporations are really earning enormously larger sums ON THEIR BASIC INVESTMENTS?

If they turn to the small co-operative corporation, issuing common stock and explaining its real possibilities, are they not "headed off" by magazine articles that solemnly warn them that "6 per cent and safety" are synonymous?

Is there not, in short, a concerted, highly developed and skillfully planned capitalistic system in force that COMPELS the people's savings into channels arranged by the system?

Let us repeat: The remedy is education, knowledge, UNDERSTANDING. Let the present structures of "high finance" stand. Let the people, acting with due caution and intelligence, turn their funds into corporations with their ORIGINAL capitalization intact, purchasing their stock under conditions where the dividends earned are distributed in full, and in common, among all the shareholders in exact proportion to their holdings.

Then, they will RECEIVE exactly and precisely what their money EARNS.

Recognize the fact that a bank is a custodian of your funds—not an investment agent for them. Use it as you would your pocket—as a container for funds ordinarily required. Set your SURPLUS to work, really to WORK. Let no middleman take nineteen-twentieths of the fruit of your labor. That is the road that leads to fortune.

DISCOURSE XI.

INJURIOUS DOCTRINE OF CAPITALISTS.

The previous article demonstrated conclusively two great facts:

First: That the earning power of the people's money is about nineteen-twentieths greater than what they actually receive.

Second: That the members of a small group or "clique," comprising the owners of about one hundred gigantic corporations, are taking these nineteen-twentieths.

Let us now draw a labor and investment parallel:

Labor contends, and rightly, that it creates wealth. From this fundamental viewpoint, labor has always been more or less dissatisfied with the share in the form of WAGES that has been given it of the wealth it has created.

Since the eighteenth century, labor has enforced its demands by means of strikes, rendered possible by the offensive of trade unions.

Without discussing the rights or wrongs of the labor question, or discussing special cases that have either caused criticism or justified themselves in the eyes of the world, a great fact may be pointed out:

Since the eighteenth century labor has undoubtedly improved its possession. By an intelligent analysis of his position in industry and commerce, the laboring man has, through united action, forced capitalists to yield him a larger share of the wealth he assists in creating.

He has, as a consequence, risen from a condition that closely approached mere serfdom, to a position where he secures, as a right and birthright, some of the comforts and pleasures, if not luxuries, of life.

There is no doubt that the condition of labor, under the stimulus of education, will continue to improve. There is very little doubt that, eventually, labor will not alone draw a fixed and remunerative wage, but will also draw part of the profits from the business enterprises it assists in building.

That day, indeed, is already with us. We see it demonstrated partially, at least, in the Ford Motor Company's plant, in the plant of the United States Steel Corporation, and in numerous enterprises that have placed their business on a coöperative basis, giving to labor a share in the profits earned.

This concession has been FOUGHT for. It has not been dowered as a voluntary gift. The condition has been brought about as a result

of intelligent thinking and analysis on the part of workingmen. It is a beginning, and the whole body of labor is moving to better and greater things.

Even now the laborer must take largely what the employer offers. Necessity compels it. On the other hand, the man with money to spare has been taking largely what the capitalist offered, without being driven to it. Compulsion has ruled with labor, sophistry with savings. Both labor and capital undoubtedly have been ruled in different ways by HIGHER INTELLECT. The men who now own one-seventh of this country's resources are undoubtedly CLEVER. We must concede that point when we recognize what they have accomplished.

They have shaped law and sentiment to further their own ends, and under many cloaks of subtlety and sophistry have secured the funds of the people until today the country is being raked to get even the pennies that the children save, and those pennies go voluntarily and WILLINGLY to further swell already swollen fortunes, and to further expand what is now nearly unlimited financial power.

Americans are cleverly hypnotized. As Samuel Untermeyer, the noted New York lawyer, stated in the New York Annalist:

"There is nothing on earth so inert and gullible as the average American investor. He lacks the most primitive instinct of self-preservation. The same group of financial buccaneers can exploit him with impunity, just as often as they choose, by a trifling shift in the machinery each time. The whole equipment consists of a few names of men who represent financial power and a press bureau."

To which may be added that the "press bureau" is probably the chief factor.

Today the American investor, when it comes to a wise disposition of his funds, is as far back as labor was in the eighteenth century when serfdom was accepted as the lot of labor. The lot of the laborer was then hard. He was exploited by capital because he knew no better. He was bound in voluntary chains and accepted what was offered—not what he could have gotten. The saving classes of today accept what is offered—not what they can get. Hard necessity compelled labor to enter into a hard agreement, but that condition does not rule the saver. The latter is under no necessity to take what is offered. His enslavement has been brought about in a more subtle way. He feels he SHOULD take it—that it is best for him—that the men "who live in a higher sphere" are guardians of his financial destiny. He is simply enslaved by the customs of deep rooted financial HABIT.

Today no investor would buy a bond without the words: "Payable in gold of the present standard of weight and fineness"; and no giant corporation would dare put out bonds without these words, because CUSTOM dictates that these words shall be used. If the American investor will DEMAND more he will get more. If he does not get what he demands he will not be embarrassed, as he is a free agent and can put his funds to work in investment channels outside those formed by the hundred or so corporations that, through the savings banks, the life insurance companies and the bond houses, take the bulk of the savings of the American public.

Why should we elect to deliver the property and resources of this country into the hands of a hundred millionaires? Why should we consent to allow them to take the fruits of our labor? Why should all other corporations outside of this group have to go hat in hand to this hundredgroup if they wish to develop some natural resource or opportunity? WHY? There is no reason, except the force of habit and custom by which Americans have been enthralled.

Representative Collier of Mississippi, in a speech in the House against interlocking directorates, declared that the Southern Railroad had to go to J. P. Morgan & Company with an exorbitant premium to get money with which to meet $50,000,000 of bonds about to fall due.

"They are straining every nerve to pay the enormous interest on that great bonded indebtedness of theirs", said Mr. Collier. "They cannot pay those bonds, so they have to go to J. P. Morgan & Company and get $50,000,000 to redeem those bonds. The Morgan Company says: 'We will give you $50,000,000, but we want $60,000,000 for this $50,000,000 of bonds; we want you to add $10,000,000 more in bonds.'

"The people in Mississippi, Alabama, Georgia, Florida and the Carolinas, Tennessee, Virginia and Kentucky", he said, "are paying the freight and giving Morgan & Company more than $10,000,000, and have to pay the interest on those bonds."

It is a popular belief that the giant capitalists of America are content with from 4 to 5 per cent on their money. Approach them with such a proposition and they will scoff at you. They want more—much more—and they see to it that they get it. True, they buy 4 or 5 per cent bonds at a big discount, and sell them to the public at par, or better. But they also take a bonus of ten or twenty millions in bonds for their aid. What do they really make? Is it 4 or 5 per cent?

One has but to piece together the meagre items of information that appear occasionally in the financial press to realize what a tremendous confidence game is being worked on the American people by those "behind the scenes", rendered possible only by the customs and habits of the people themselves, who deliberately play into the hands that are gradually, but nevertheless most securely, enslaving them.

Within an incredibly short span the lands of America, the funds of America, the credit of America will drift into the hands of an exceeding small clique of men who will hold the country under bond and mortgage. Then we will have a form of aristocracy like that of England where large landholders are the ruling power. The thing is on its way now with the giant strides of seven league boots, and its accomplishment is inevitable unless Americans wake up to the monetary peril that threatens them and change their investment habits.

The remedy is simple. Stop buying bonds—stop buying limited preferred stocks—demand that shares of stock be issued bearing the statement that the purchasers are entitled to share in all the earnings that the company makes. Then, in place of a hundred or a thousand millionaires, we will have hundreds of thousands, yes millions, of wealthy contented people, because the true productiveness of this marvelous land will be evenly distributed, pro rata with the investment made, TO THE PEOPLE OF AMERICA—not to a hundred corporations.

Begin today—preach the creed to your neighbor—enjoin him to preach it to his neighbor—let the endless chain of financial enlightenment get to work, and the financial fabric that now takes nineteen-twentieths of the earnings belonging to the people must collapse. Nor will its collapse harm. The "game" will simply stop, and the powers that be will be compelled to give the people what they are rightfully entitled to. That is the true "remedy" for the ills that afflict us.

And now let us examine a few fallacies preached through the subsidized or "kept" financial press and see what they amount to.

A small corporation is formed on an OPPORTUNITY—a patent or a process, perhaps. It has no assets, as assets are commonly termed; that is, it has no real estate, or rentals, or income.

It is "attacked" on this account as a "bubble" corporation. But is it? It has capitalized a POTENTIALITY at a sum absurdly beneath its intrinsic worth if it makes good. This suppositious corporation, when formed, has shares of stock to sell—as much a commodity as goods in a manufacturer's warehouse; it has to face a selling expense, precisely as a manufacturer would. In commercial transactions this selling expense (from 25 to 50 per cent) is added to the cost of the goods, but in the transaction of selling the shares in the corporation it very seldom is. On the other hand, the shares are frequently offered at a DISCOUNT.

The sponsors appreciate the value of their opportunity. They know what the real power of money is, and they make sacrifices of all kinds to get it. Very frequently they "baby" the company along by accepting no salaries, or only nominal salaries, until success has been demonstrated. Frequently they offer the public preferred shares that take the first earnings of the company, being themselves content with common shares that draw no dividends until the dividends on the preferred shares have been earned and paid. At times they go even further and let the preferred shareholders participate equally with the holders of common shares in the profits that remain after the dividends on the preferred shares have been paid.

They make, in short, SACRIFICIAL CONCESSIONS to get dollars—the dollars which they know, if once gotten, will earn hundreds or thousands per cent. Watching their efforts, the "kept" financial press jeers at them as "irresponsible" and "bubble" corporations, while pointing to its own giant concerns with ample assets and income, and telling the people to be "safe" and buy their 4 or 5 per cent bonds.

So Gordon McKay, of the McKay Sewing Machine Association, ostracized by the bankers to whom he would not give control, was forced to peddle his stock among the poor cotton workers of Lowell and to the hardy whaling population of New Bedford—forced to sacrificial concessions he knew should not be made, but had to be made to get those precious dollars he needed. When he got them, and got them to work, the first dividend declared made those poor people wealthy.

Take the Dunlop Company, formed on a patent. Lacking assets of any kind, it nevertheless had a tremendous potentiality under its hand in the protection afforded by the country to the invention. Without wealth, it was marvelously rich. It had an opportunity. The capital was $112,000. When the precious dollars needed were painfully scraped together by great self-denial and sacrifice, and those dollars got to WORK, what happened? In two years the company was sold for $15,000,000 cash. Even in that short period the original shareholders had received in dividends and premiums the sum of $3,290,575, and by the terms of the sale received a further sum of $14,437,500 —$17,728,075 for $112,000 in two years—$158 for $1—7,900 per cent a year profit.

What happened to the thought of a brain when visualized by the Bessemer steel process? The inventor was jeered down when he asked for capital outside of financing circles; but he fought for it, sold "a little stock" to one open-minded person and took the first step towards financing what netted that openminded person some ten million dollars, and gave the world a process whose worth billions of dollars would be required to measure.

What is the choice given such men? Either to go to the bankers and lose their birthright, or go to the public and fight the antagonistic subsidized press—to fight established habit and custom and the people's lack of financial knowledge, or sacrifice their opportunity for a mess of pottage.

Thus we see the tremendous PRESSURE exercised by the present financial system to reap the fruits of every endeavor, whether the system is entitled to it or not.

What is the end and aim? To make those in need of financing to come to the bankers—to make those whose aggregate funds could do the financing also to come to the bankers.

And to the bankers the majority of them go. A railroad gives up $10,000,000 for their aid. An inventor gives up as many millions for their help. The public, through the whole damnable system, gives up billions it might possess.

But the system is defeating itself. Formerly it "stood in" and shared the spoils with a larger "clique". Now it has grown so strong, and is so entrenched, that it divides nothing and demands all.

This item recently appeared in the New York World:

"The public offering of the Third Avenue Railroad Company was made yesterday without the services of a Wall Street underwriting syndicate, and proved so successful that other corporations will undoubtedly be induced to adopt this economical method of financing."

And "other corporations", tired of usurious exactions, have also seen the light. The New York Tribune, of May 28th, 1915, carried the announcement of the Interborough Metropolitan Company, containing this significant phrase:

"It is intended that, if approved, the plan shall be carried out without the intervention of any syndicate or bankers and without payment of commissions."

Recently the city of Chicago got tired of the exaction of the bankers and syndicates and underwriters and offered its bonds at par direct to the people with wonderful success. The people got the bonds at par instead of at a premium as heretofore, and the city received the par value of them without any expense of commission or discount or bonus. The financiers didn't like this plan, but the bond buyers and taxpayers did.

The larger corporations outside the "clique" are not giving up $10,000,000 or so for financial accommodations, and the public is supporting the corporations that refuse the hold-up, recognizing that in the end the country pays under a perpetual exaction of interest or dividends payable on the bonus the members of the clique create for themselves.

Still the public buys the BONDS of these corporations.

The next step is to recognize the people's RIGHT to shares of stock that give back, in proportion to the investment, ALL THAT

THE MONEY PAID FOR THOSE SHARES EARNS. This is the road to financial liberation.

Save. Then invest in young corporations that have to GROW and create wealth AS they grow. Be a partner, not a creditor, in the enterprise. Dollars breed. See that the progeny comes to you—not to a small clique whose only claim to it is that of having thrown dust in the eyes of those who make the clique possible.

DISCOURSE XII.

SPREADING THE MONEY NET.

Sometimes you will see a product advertised in the newspapers without any name or address attached, such as Pear's Soap, Wilson's Whisky, Babbitt's Cleanser, etc. The advertisement simply tells you that you may get the product "at all stores". Behind such an announcement you know that there must be a big business and a thorough distributing system, because the advertiser is apparently indifferent as to which store you go as long as you go to SOME store. In other words, every store in the country carries his product, and no matter where you purchase the advertiser will get the benefit of your purchase.

You may ask for Babbitt's Cleanser in some giant department store in New York, or in some remote California village—you will get it at both places, and both stores, big and little, will pay their legitimate commercial tribute to B. T. Babbitt, Inc., of New York. B. T. Babbitt, Inc., will get the major portion of the nickel you pay, no matter where or how you pay it. This, of course, is absolutely and perfectly legitimate; good value is given for the money, and B. T. Babbitt, Inc., is therefore rendering a public service. Reference here to this well known preparation is simply made for illustrative purposes. An enormous sign, costing thousands of dollars, may simply say "Buy Babbitt's Cleanser", and you may go to any store and buy it, and B. T. Babbitt, Inc., will get its profit just as certainly and just as surely as if you went to its New York warehouse and paid your nickel there. It is a matter of absolute indifference to B. T. Babbitt, Inc., where you buy Babbitt's Cleanser, so long as you DO buy it.

Keep this commercial transaction carefully in mind, because presently it will shed an illuminating light on what follows.

John Moody published some years ago a book entitled "The Truth About the Trusts". Mr. Moody has had ample opportunities for studying these vast aggregations of capital, as he has published "Moody's Manual of Corporation Securities" and "Moody's Bureau of Corporation Statistics". In other words, Mr. Moody is an authority on this trust subject.

On the first page of this book Mr. Moody drew a copyrighted chart which he termed "The Rockefeller-Morgan 'Family Tree', Showing the Concentration, Alliance and Interdependence of the Great Financial, Commercial and Industrial Interests of the United States."

DISCOURSE XII.

When we look at this chart we see in the centre two large squares, one representing the Standard Oil group, and the other the Morgan group. These squares are connected by lines with little circles and oblongs, representing industries.

We see the Rockefeller group connected with:
Public Service Corporations,
Telephone Interests,
Telegraph Interests,
Franchise Groups,
Railroads,
Independent Allied Lines,
Smelter Trusts,
Ice and Oil Trusts,
Tobacco Trust, and
Subsidiary Companies.
And we see the Morgan group connected with:
Franchise Groups,
Lighting Interests,
Railroads,
Pennsylvania Railroad,
Smaller Allied Lines,
Industrial Trusts,
General Electric Company,
Rubber Trust,
United States Steel Corporation,
Shipping Trust,
Subsidiary Companies, etc.

WHAT WE SEE IS THAT TWO SMALL GROUPS OF MEN, CLASSED AS THE "ROCKEFELLER GROUP" AND THE "MORGAN GROUP", ARE DIRECTLY OR INDIRECTLY INTERESTED VITALLY IN ABOUT EVERY LARGE BUSINESS ENTERPRISE IN THE COUNTRY.

We see that they do not care where you invest a dollar, or a thousand dollars, or a hundred thousand dollars, so long as you invest it in "seasoned securities".

We see that, as a great rule, when you do invest, your money goes into either the Rockefeller or the Morgan group.

WE WILL SEE LATER THAT WHEN IT GOES TO ONE OF THESE GROUPS IT GOES UNDER CONDITIONS WHERE THE "CLIQUE" WHO COMPRISES IT GETS NINETEEN-TWENTIETHS OF ITS EARNING POWER, AND YOU GET BUT ONE-TWENTIETH.

We will see that there is a perfected financial system that, by and through the magazines and newspapers, by and through the banks, by and through the reportorial agencies, by and through the insurance and other companies, leads, coaxes and drives the dollars of the masses to this "clique" of the classes as assuredly and as certainly as if these dollars were wrenched from them by force.

We will see how the members of this basically small "clique", growing stupendously rich and powerful, are wresting money rights from the people right under their eyes by a species of financial hypnotism that makes the victims think they are being taken care of in lieu of being fleeced.

We will see what giant forces this "clique" applies in its ambitious task of mortgaging, and thus enslaving, a hundred million people.

We will see the very forces of LAW moulded and used to further this purpose. We will see the press subsidized and the people hypnotized by this subtle system of aggrandizement that the "clique" is working to dominate the masses. We will see the dollars passing into the hands of a few, and those few controlling with those dollars, directly or indirectly, the sources of POWER—the army, the navy, the press. We will see what little show the people have, should they see the fetters binding them and endeavor to break them. We will show many things that appear right to the ordinary man, simply because he has never dug down to the basic ideas that govern them.

Consider these facts:

By every conceivable appeal and device the people are urged:

To be thrifty—to save money.

For that purpose savings banks are established.

And life insurance companies are operated.

And bond investments are provided.

The people are treated with paternal care—warned against incurring "risk" with their funds.

Magazines and newspapers devote special columns, voluntarily, to urge the people to invest in "sound" bonds of "sound" business enterprises.

All these are undisputed facts.

Well, the people are "thrifty"—their funds go into savings banks. Where do the funds of the savings banks go? Into approved bond issues. Who issue "approved" bond issues? Corporations like the Pennsylvania Railroad and kindred institutions—the "clique" comprising the Rockefeller and Morgan groups. The "clique" holds the shares of stock, and the public holds the bonds.

The shares of stock are "watered", "watered", "watered" to hide the real profits. Why are the real profits HIDDEN? Why do the members of the "clique" not appear as directors and officers of the vast organizations they control through their holdings of stock? Simply because if these things were broad and open and clear the public would not, could not, stand for the menace a single day.

In other words, the "jig" would be up.

And that, in very plain words, is what every great financier knows deep down in his heart.

Ask yourself these questions:

Who moulded and enacted the COMPULSURY laws FORCING savings banks to invest their funds in BONDS?

Were those laws moulded and enacted in the interest of the people, or in the interest of the "clique"?

Why do the magazines urge investment in bonds? Are not these very magazines subsidized, owned and controlled by the "clique", or supported in their advertising columns by the bond houses? If they induce you to buy certain bonds, must not your funds go, as certainly as the nickel you pay for Babbitt's Cleanser goes to B. T. Babbitt, Inc., into the bond broker's hands first, and into the hands of the "clique" last?

You are told a Pennsylvania Railroad bond is safe. It is, undoubtedly. So you buy it. Whom do you benefit? First, the magazine that worked up the sale by its recommendation. It has your order and other orders to show as a result of its influence and standing. Consequently it receives advertising revenue, not from the "clique" direct, but from jobbers, or brokers or agents OF the "clique".

A little of your money stays with the bond house through which you made the purchase. Its discount or commission is small enough, and will hurt no one. The great fact is that the major portion—the greater portion of your investment—drops into the bank account of the "clique", even though it has passed through a dozen more ostensible channels on its way there.

This represents a voluntary purchase. But you often purchase involuntarily; as for instance, when your bank, which operates on your money and the money of thousands of others like you, buys, BY LEGAL COMPULSION, the bonds of companies that the "clique" controls.

You buy involuntarily when your life insurance company buys, BY LEGAL COMPULSION, bonds of the companies that the "clique" controls.

Don't be misled by custom. Question custom, and you will get some startling facts.

The Department of Commerce, Washington,

D. C., in a bulletin recently issued, shows that "In the period since 1870, the value of our farm products has risen from 2 billion to about 10 billion dollars a year; the output of coal from less than 30 to nearly 500 million long tons; copper from 12½ thousand to over one-half million tons; pig iron from 2 to 31 million tons; petroleum from 221 million to 9¼ billion gallons; and manufactures from 4 billion to over 20 billion dollars."

All of which sounds very interesting and very prosperous, until we ask:

Who owns the coal mines?

Who owns the copper mines?

Who owns the petroleum fields?

Who owns the iron deposits?

And those who know will answer back: "Well, the larger ownership vests in Amalgamated, U. S. Steel, and Standard Oil."

And if we push that question a little further we will find that the men who control those corporations through the ownership of shares of stock—not bonds, oh, no—comprise the "clique" forming the Rockefeller and Morgan groups.

And we find that while the wealth of the United States in 1850 was $7,135,780,000, and in 1914 $107,104,212,000, yet, by some mysterious process, the wealth of the people has not increased individually in proportion with the aggregate gain, but that the wealth of a comparatively small group or "clique" has increased stupendously.

Invisible hands reached out through that interval of time and took to themselves the collective wealth as it was created. By fine, subtle processes, too complex for the average brain to follow, the man whose dollar earned another dollar in the course of the year found himself GETTING but 5 cents, 4 cents or 3 cents. He could never advance, but the "clique" that created the tools—bonds—on which he used his money, advanced so fast that the recital of its gains is one of the most marvelous chapters of business history.

Still, when you look at things fairly and squarely, through the glasses of truth, is the game difficult to see through? In reality, it is exceedingly simple. Men will HOARD money—that is a natural tendency, one of the strongest of human nature.

Very well; find them a safe place to hoard it—a bank—and even pay them a little for the privilege of taking care of it—a bank, of course, does not keep such money in its safe or vault, but lends it. Then pass a law compelling these banks to invest in certain classes of bonds, and as we own these bonds, when the banks need them, to comply with the law, the money of the people, deposited in the banks, must be sent by the banks to us, because we have a law compelling them either to keep the money in their vaults—where it would be useless to them —or to buy our bonds with it.

So our bonds are sold, and we get the major portion of the cash, whether the bonds are bought in California or in New York, and whether the people save and buy them direct from us, or save and put their money in the bank and the bank buys them. In other words, we have a "corner" on the bonds available for legal investment. The bonds specified by the Government ARE OUR BONDS, and anyone who buys, or who buys for third parties, must eventually, and most assuredly, COME TO US.

We take that bond money on which we pay, say, 5 per cent, and put it into productive and constructive channels where it makes HUNDREDS PER CENT.

We get nearly all of these hundreds per cent —we the "clique"—because our bonds only draw 5 per cent.

Isn't it all perfectly simple?

All this, of course, is accomplished by leading the people to deposit their money in savings banks, and then compelling the savings banks to invest in our bonds. So far it is all very simple.

But what of the man who won't deposit his money in savings banks? What of the man who thinks his money ought to earn more than savings banks give?

Well, we'll admit the soundness of his argument and viewpoint. We will use no force or coercion—at least none that he can perceive. We will direct his mind involuntarily, unconsciously. By leading him to believe himself a free agent, he will really be doing what we want him to do. Doing what we want him to do for our own selfish interests, he will believe we are taking a philanthropic interest in his welfare.

We will get his money just as certainly and just as surely as we COMPEL that of the savings banks.

How?

Because we are powerful enough to subsidize, control, or prove profitable the things this man trusts, and the things that shape and form his mind conceptions. He reads to gain information and knowledge. Through what he reads our gospel will be preached. His favorite newspaper and his trusted periodical will tell him that money cannot with safety earn more than 5 per cent. They will urge him with fatherly care to buy "approved bonds" and to regard stocks as things of evil.

In this way we follow the true mind processes of one of the "clique".

"But", you may say, "while your plans seem comprehensive, and pretty sure to succeed, there still remains a type of man who will refuse to believe that 4 or 5 per cent is all that he can expect his money to earn. That man will escape you."

"Not so quick", the "clique" representative will reply. "We cover his type of mind, too. He is a 'speculator'—a financial adventurer—and to get his money we must cater to him."

"And how", you ask, "is that done?"

"Through Wall Street and the Stock Exchange", comes answer. "Here the man who sees that he who gets wealthy is the one who buys shares of stock, will be tendered shares, and, while apparently free and a free agent, his money will just as surely reach our—the 'clique's'—coffers."

"How?"

"Because we will show him a stock that is rising in value. After he has purchased it the price will fall. It will fall so low that he will be discouraged and sell it. We sold him the stock at a high price. We will buy it back at the low price. He paid us $1,000 for ten shares.

After a year he sold us those ten shares for $600. As the shares have always been worth par, it is evident we have made $400 by the transaction. Within a week you will see those shares selling at par, or better, and we can repeat the operation again and again."

"But this man will eventually become discouraged and draw out of Wall Street."

"Assuredly! Disgusted with speculation, he will resolve to SAVE his money in the future. Whatever he does, we have him, going and coming. That is why we are money princes."

"Is there, then, no way this man may really put his money out and honestly receive what it earns?"

"Well, there is, but naturally we're not advertising it—in fact, we 'hammer' it—the less he knows of it the better. Why, man, that would mean financial liberation, and we want no such propaganda as that. Our chains are around this man, though he is unaware of them. WE WANT THE FRUITS OF HIS LIFE TO COME TO US. We want him to earn a living, assuredly, but what he earns over and above that living must go, shall go, to support our social fabric—the members of the "clique"—that ride and race and yacht and drive in pleasure and splendor their whole lives through."

DISCOURSE XIII.

A NATION DELUDED.

There is national as well as individual hypnotism. One has but to read history to find that all people and all governments have been or are under the spell of misconceptions and delusions—following will-o'-the-wisps that have led or are leading them into quagmires of difficulties which invariably terminate in untold sacrifice of life and wealth.

One delusion that the people of many nations have ever suffered from has been a specious APPEARANCE of freedom; apparently they were free agents, able and willing to do as they chose; apparently the ills that afflicted them were unescapable ills, things with which Providence afflicted them and that had to be stoically endured. Under this delusion of free will, people have gone down into conditions closely approximating slavery and bondage. Each man has felt that no other man was interfering with his individual struggles and exertions, and that, as a consequence, the handicaps or privations from which he suffered were things that neither he nor his fellows could avoid. The masses have been told by people who have been as much subject to this delusion as themselves, and who, therefore, were thoroughly sincere and thoroughly in earnest, to be sober, hard-working, thrifty and frugal.

Men, naturally, should be sober, hard working, thrifty and frugal; but there are degrees of these things, and if we believe that these virtues ALONE will carry us to wealth and happiness, WE ARE VERY MUCH MISTAKEN. Something else is required.

That "something else" is not PHYSICAL, but MENTAL freedom. We must learn to realize that keen, subtle brains have woven a mental mesh around us, so invisible, and yet so strong, that we are prisoners within it, and will remain such until we break through it by force of INDEPENDENT THINKING.

The average man follows his fellows, not only physically but mentally. In other words, men THINK IN DROVES. A few lead and the rest follow, just as sheep jump the hurdle that the leader jumps.

This tendency to adopt and follow ready-made thought has its good and evil sides. It is good for the multitude when its thinkers lead them right, but bad when they lead them astray. It may be set down as an axiom that sooner or later capital captures the men who think, and so colors their mentality that they think along the lines capital wishes. The rewards are all on that side, and when the mass fights the class the mental conditions are unequal, for, almost invariably, the class wins. If we could see the victory or defeat in the ending, we would at least know what was going on; but the trouble is that the class scores without APPEARING to do so.

The people are either led or driven, but in either case they go, AS A MASS, the way that the subtle brains that control them want them to go.

In the preceding article, "Spreading the Money Net," it was indicated conclusively that money rules the world; that knowledge is power, and power is money; and MONEY GETS EVERYTHING IT WANTS.

THE MEN WHO CAN GET THE MONEY OF THE PEOPLE GET ALL THEY WANT.

Now, reader, pause and reflect carefully, and see if a FEW men are not getting the people's money.

Apparently you are a free agent, but let us see if you really are. You desire to save money. You have not the means to surround that money with steel bars and electrical vaults, so you take it to men who have those means, and who you know are honest enough to return it to you when you ask for it—in other words, you take it to a savings bank. In doing this you are acting, apparently, as a free agent. You have been COAXED to take it there, certainly; but you have not been FORCED to take it there.

However, at this point sit down and think hard. Analyze your mental processes, if you can. You are taking, say $1,000 to the savings bank. You will get $30 from that bank for the use of that thousand dollars for one year.

If you have read the previous article in this book, you KNOW, surely and emphatically KNOW, that that thousand dollars will earn SOMEONE ELSE from four hundred to six hundred dollars during the year.

Who is that "someone" else? "The bank", perhaps you answer; but that would not be necessarily right, and might be very far wrong. For the nonce, we will assume that you have not been influenced to take that money to the bank, but when that money gets in the bank, THE BANK ITSELF is FORCED to put that money into certain specified channels of investment, and that if you will follow it in its tortuous course, you will find that the centre of the vortex to which it ultimately swirls comprises what is known as "the Morgan and Rockefeller groups".

DISCOURSE XIII.

If you could follow the work of this "crowd" you would see that through banks, trust companies, insurance companies, etc., etc., they are obligated to return back to the people stupendous sums of money—so stupendous that we will not consider the figures, because in all probability your brain simply could not grasp them.

You would find that if the people, en masse, should demand their money back, these men, great and powerful as they are, would go to smash overnight; because they could not give back a fourth of what they take through forms of law, and remain solvent.

Isn't that the whole story? Can't you SEE that they cannot be working with their own money, because if they were they could repay dollar for dollar? Is it not easy to see that not only are they working with the people's money, but that they are working with all of it so completely that if the people demanded it overnight they would be powerless to give it back to them?

We are now getting down to crude, raw, elemental thought conceptions, because that is where the truth lays—stripped of all subtleties, that is the situation.

Now THINK and think HARD. Has it ever happened that these men have been called on by the people, en masse, to give them back their money? It surely has. What happened? The people were calmly told that IT COULDN'T BE DONE. They were told in effect that the promises of these men "to pay in gold of the present standard of weight and fineness" was, to drop into the expressive vernacular, so much "bunk" and "hot air".

Don't forget that. While a few people ask for their money, they get it; but when they all ask, they do not get it.

This is exactly what occurs when a so-called "panic" runs through the country. The people are fed on optimism until the diet reacts on them, when they begin to distrust the ability of these men to deliver to them what they have contracted to deliver, AND THEY ASK FOR THEIR MONEY.

What happens? The people simply can't get their money. The savings banks take their legal time limit and refuse to pay out their cash. The commercial banks "short cut" the whole matter by closing their doors. Where is the money "to be paid in gold of the present standard of weight and fineness"? Where is the bank credit upon which you have been accustomed to draw? It simply, literally, and most emphatically ISN'T THERE.

DISCOURSE XIII.

Where is it? In the ultimate, in a few vaults of a few men in Wall Street. When it comes to a "show down", that's where the money is found, and from those few vaults, owned by a few men, comes the money that—"RETRIEVES THE COUNTRY AND QUELLS THE PANIC".

You know this is true. It is raw elemental truth. The situation really is an exquisite farce, as the people, when their own money is put up to quell the panic and save the country, acclaim with cries of joy and gratitude, their "savior" blessed.

The little man who lost his money in the little bank in Kokomo, or some other centre, isn't saved; but some of the people are saved all the time, because it would never do to let them go utterly and completely, as would happen if some "saving" was not done. Every bit of "beef" in the country who is willing to work with his hands in lieu of his brains, is a precious asset to Wall Street financiers. And assets are valuable; hence some "saving" must be done.

And this "beef" must be kept grateful and reverential, because if it turned (as the French ultimately did in the French Revolution) brawn would master brain, and many of these deep schemers would lose their heads.

Do you get at least a glimpse of the MENTAL DOMINATION that is being exercised?

Are you really the free agent you think you are?

If you had a thousand head of cattle, would you drive them into a pen and at the end of twelve months take thirty back from the man that accepted them? You would not, because the transaction would be too apparently, far too obviously, a snare, delusion and cheat.

All right—another man offers you the 300 to 400 calves the herd will produce by the end of the year. The first man cries, "You take a risk—you take a risk." You hesitate, believe him, and drive the cattle to his pen—not for a year, but for your whole life. You are as "beefy" as your cattle. You have not brains enough to understand that your cattle will breed and multiply to the same extent no matter which man has them. Because you are not only "beefy" but a mental coward, you let the second man take from you what should rightly be yours.

Your neighbors follow your example. Soon this man owns enormous herds, and you and your neighbors own very small herds. You revere him as a master mind—as a man who is so infinitely clever that he makes more than you, as a matter of course—literally you believe he moves "in a higher sphere".

He has his friends, favorites and sycophants, of course; and soon you see the clique around him also owning enormous herds, while you and your neighbors still own very small herds. Naturally, you esteem these men for their cleverness and skill.

Soon reporters, apparently on behalf of the people, will interview these men, asking the secret of their success. And these men will solemnly advise the people to scrimp and save until they get from ten to a hundred head of cattle, which they are then to drive to these huge cattle pens and get "interest" on them in the form of three calves a year for every hundred they drive in.

Soon these men who own these vast herds can bestow cattle freely on men who do their bidding.

The masses delegate their governing functions to magistrates and judges, to politicians and editors, etc., giving them meagre compensation in the shape of cattle.

The classes—comprising the big cattle holders—advertiser in the editors' publications, giving them large cattle donations for the space they buy. The judges and politicians are continuously favored in the same way. Soon certain obstacles are thrown in the way of doing a cattle pen business, and only the favorites of the "class" can do it. True, the field, APPARENTLY, is open to all, but when the outsider steps forward he finds that he must have cattle in large numbers to perpetuate the cattle gain; and as he has BEEN GIVING UP HIS CATTLE to the cattle kings, he fails on the first necessary qualification.

But, perhaps, by toil, thrift and work this man has "saved" cattle—paid a heavy price in toil and anxiety, and done it. He complies with the law that the judges and magistrates, the editors and politicians have made to keep him out, and he, too, begins to run a cattle pen.

If so, he becomes a factor in the community, certainly a man to respect—a man to be respected. But as the cattle come to his pen HE MUST DRIVE THEM TO ANOTHER PEN —the law says so, and DEMANDS SO. These cattle, representing the savings of the people, go from pen to pen and pen to pen, each pen getting gradually bigger and more capacious, until they get to the Wall Street pen, WHERE THEY GO NO FARTHER.

When the country, in the throes of a panic, is mad with the fear that its resources are sapped and its credit bankrupt—when the ignorant herdsmen from far and near are for once DEMANDING their cattle—these cattle are trotted out before their vision as the property of another man, to reassure them, to show them that the wealth of the country is still within it. This man may even put up forty or fifty million head to assist the other cattle pens. The people prostrate themselves before him, and call him blessed.

The country is saved; people THINK their money is safe once again; "confidence is restored", and they don't all ask for their cattle again. If they did, they wouldn't get them.

Verily, a NATION DELUDED.

The crux of the whole matter and the remedy lay in this thought:

A DOLLAR (APPROXIMATELY) REPRESENTS THE LABOR OF ONE MAN FOR AN ENTIRE DAY, AND $300 HIS LABOR FOR AN ENTIRE YEAR. ON THIS $300 THE SYSTEM WILL PAY 3 PER CENT. THE "INTEREST" SYSTEM DECLARES THAT LABOR IS ONLY CAPABLE OF PRODUCING $9 FOR THE WHOLE YEAR. COMMON SENSE TELLS US THAT IF WE SET A MAN ON ANY CONSTRUCTIVE WORK NEEDED BY THE WORLD FOR A WHOLE YEAR, HE WILL EARN INFINITELY MORE.

Let us take an elemental case—a man cutting cord wood. A good woodsman will cut and stack a cord a day; that wood, in the open market, is worth an average of $1.25 a cord, or 300 cords are worth $375. AT THE CRUDEST AND LOWEST FORM OF LABOR THE LABORER PRODUCES THAT SUM OF MONEY AS THE PRODUCT OF A YEAR'S WORK.

Remember this—

WHEN YOU ARE TOLD THAT THE DOLLAR IS INCAPABLE OF DOING WHAT THE MAN DOES, YOU ARE BEING TOLD A LIVING LIE.

Money is simply labor; money buys labor; the greater the skill in labor bought, the greater the returns. When a natural opportunity is developed, labor is required to reap its fruits. YOUR DOLLARS ARE CONTINUALLY BUYING THIS LABOR EFFORT, and the returns, averaged, are infinitely greater than the product of the woodsman we have cited; yet, under the present system, WHILE THE MASSES DEVELOP THE COUNTRY THE CLASSES ACQUIRE ITS OWNERSHIP.

Look at this stark, naked truth and fact and grasp what it means if you can. It means others are acquiring your birthright. It means that invisible hands grasp your production and whisk it from you. It means that you die poor while they die rich. It means life is a heaven to them and something very different to you. It means that people live in riotous sumptuousness on the West Side, while they die and rot in poverty and disease on the East Side.

We attack no individual or group of individuals. We attack a world FALLACY. We simply state a fact. We seek to bring light to a nation deluded.

Labor has long been aware of the fact that brains were exploiting it, but labor has never perceived the method. In some way, the things LABOR CREATED were, at the end, found in the hands of others. It was all very mysterious, all very baffling, and all, apparently, right and regular. Labor simply knew it was aiming at or fighting SOMETHING that was grievously wounding it. It was all a baffling mystery.

LABOR MUST SEE TO IT THAT IT IS CAPITALIZED, AND THE EARNINGS OF THAT CAPITALIZATION RETURNED TO IT.

Isn't it all very simple? An opportunity is found. Money is required to develop it. Money is simply frozen labor. This exhilarating fuel is thrown into the enterprise, moving the wheels that produce new, clean, bloodless wealth. This wealth is the product of the frozen labor (money) that has been saved. EVERY CENT OF IT BELONGS TO THE MEN WHO PUT IT INTO THE OPPORTUNITY, and back to them it should come in exact proportion to what each has put in.

Labor will fight the capitalistic genii in vain while it seeks to COMPEL them to divide as they justly should. Labor has simply to IGNORE them to get what it justly should.

Let labor wipe the "savings", "bond" and "speculative" delusions from its mind, and face the fact that, producing the wealth, it should equitably SHARE the wealth produced.

Let labor utilize the corporate idea FOR labor; let it take its "savings" and invest them in shares of stock of new enterprises, under conditions where ALL THE PROFITS come back to ALL THE SHAREHOLDERS in exact proportion to their holdings, and from that moment the mysterious baffling influence that has whisked the fruits of their endeavor from their bewildered hands will no longer be felt.

Let the workers unionize their INVESTMENTS as they have unionized THEMSELVES.

Today they fight the capitalistic system, and, in the fighting, deposit in capitalistic repositories the money that enables those capitalists to maintain a system and enact laws that repress them in their fight for financial justice. They will never get anywhere while this anomaly continues.

Revolution, anarchy, socialism, interference with the material affairs of life are unnecessary if labor will but capitalize its own birthright and distribute among themselves the wealth that this country annually yields. This labor can do right here and now by supporting young and legitimate private corporations under conditions where labor will reap the full fruits of the ripened opportunity.

Let labor recognize the vital fact that there are two classes of corporations, as vital and distinct from each other as day is from night.

There is the CAPITALISTIC corporation, offering the public preferred stock or bonds—limiting opportunity.

There is the DEMOCRATIC corporation, offering shares of common stock, giving all buyers a full partnership interest in the enterprise. Such a corporation knows no discrimination. It has no "classes" among its shareholders. There are no bondholders, and there are no preferential shareholders. All are on one great democratic plane, sharing expenses and sharing profits.

MAKING MONEY MAKE MONEY.

The opportunities open to labor, union or otherwise, are legion. They are as plentiful for labor as they are for capital. Capital takes advantage of its opportunities, while labor sits with folded hands in the dismal Swamp of Despair and bemoans its fate, instead of being up and doing.

The Colorado coal strike is of such recent occurrence that its horrors are fresh in our minds. In Utah are undeveloped coal lands, containing, according to the United States Geological Survey, billions of dollars in good coal at the threshold of the market. Labor could take these lands and work for itself under conditions to receive all the profits. Labor could do this just as well as capital that will eventually do it. Then labor will do the work for capital and receive a pittance to keep body and soul together, while capital will wallow in the wealth produced. Should labor become dissatisfied, strikes and shooting and more misery will follow, but no more money for labor. IF LABOR ONLY HAD LEADERS OF DEPTH OF MIND TO COMPREHEND THE SITUATION, WHAT MIGHT NOT BE ACCOMPLISHED!

LEARN TO RECOGNIZE THE RIGHT PENS INTO WHICH TO DRIVE YOUR CATTLE.

DISCOURSE XIII.

The right pen is the coöperative pen, where the cattle are received and kept, and, as they breed and multiply, their progeny given back to the owners, less their just and ratable proportion of actual expenses.

And now—

Where are your next dollars going?

Are we right or are we wrong? If we are right, are you not doing wrong if you continue to support a system that is robbing you and yours?

If we are wrong, where, and how?

This is a good talk for your brother man, isn't it? But suppose he has the same viewpoint, and considers it a good talk FOR YOU?

The "THINKING" will never get us anywhere.

If the principles here enunciated appeal to you as RIGHT, cling fast to the truth and ACT on the truth.

Convert yourself before you attempt to convert your neighbor, and then go out and convert him.

ESTABLISH A DEMOCRACY OF INVESTMENT.

SPREAD this great propaganda.

Do this one thing, and that one thing done will make your life worth while, if you do nothing else to make it worth while.

MAKING MONEY MAKE MONEY.

Start your brother THINKING.

Escape the mental net that seeks to ensare you within its meshes.

I have taught over a hundred thousand persons these truths, the things they should know; they can teach a million if they will, and that million can start a movement that will mark an epoch in the world's history.

Talk about it to those you know.

DISCOURSE XIV.

LABOR AND MONEY ARE SYNONYMOUS.

Perhaps it will be conceded at this stage that so far two propositions have been demonstrated conclusively, namely:

1. That money is frozen labor.

2. That labor is more productive than capital concedes.

This money question will be much clearer to you if you will consider that money has the power at all times to go into the market and command labor and reap the fruits of that labor.

The man with a dollar has command of some man's time for a day.

The man with a thousand dollars has command of a thousand men's time for a day.

We speak of course of UNSKILLED labor —just crude, raw labor—labor that lays the ties and spikes down the rails of great railroads, or excavates subways beneath great cities that carry millions of souls and pay millions in dividends—of the almost universal "common" labor of the world without which the world would be a wilderness.

MAKING MONEY MAKE MONEY.

Of what use would it be for the brain to conceive a subway or a great railroad, if it lacked the hands—the millions of hard, horny hands—required to make the conception practical?

Never forget that money is useless without labor. The capitalist on a desert island, surrounded with gold bags, would be of no service to himself unless he WORKED.

Never forget that the wealth of the world—the MONEY of the world—owes its origin to, and has been created entirely by, labor.

Pause and reflect here. Study this thing carefully, because when labor grasps it the mental domination that we see in the form termed "capital" will vanish.

Labor creates the fortune of the capitalist.

Labor creates all the evidences of wealth against which securities are issued.

Labor creates the great mercantile and savings banks, the trust and insurance companies, the great railroad and steamship lines, the great telephone and telegraph systems—all these things, created by labor, BELONG BY RIGHT AND BIRTHRIGHT TO LABOR.

That labor doesn't own them is labor's fault.

What is this thing we call money?

Simply a voucher or check that society gives the bearer for "services rendered", that entitles him, on presentation, to take from the social storehouse the things he needs in the amount indicated by the voucher.

Money is nothing but a convenient tool for the exchange of wealth.

We do not strive for money, but for the things that money will get for us; and if money was swept away we would never miss it, provided we could devise as perfect a system as money gives to further the exchange of things we need.

Society asks us all to labor, and, if we do, society issues us vouchers called "bills" or "dollars" for what it judges to be the extent of our effort.

We want a blanket—we work a day for it perhaps. We want a house—we work a thousand days for it perhaps. We want a pleasure tour—we work sixty days for it perhaps. The things the world gives are gauged by LABOR, not money.

Your dollars represent labor, as you may now clearly see. You know labor is productive enough before the "capitalist" steps in, because, as was demonstrated in the preceding article, the crudest form of labor employed in cutting cordwood can cut a cord a day, worth $1.25, and that makes a wealth production through the year of 300 days, of $375.

MAKING MONEY MAKE MONEY.

Roughly speaking, a dollar a day will command a wood cutter's services, which means that you will pay him $300 and he will deliver you, at the end of the year, 300 cords of wood taken from Nature's bank, the woods.

If you had put that $300 into a bank in lieu of labor, you would have reaped 3 per cent, or $9 on your investment.

As it is, by investing it in the crudest form of labor, you have 300 cords of wood, worth approximately $375. You may not want those cords of wood, but there are others who do. Consequently you can exchange what you have for what you want. In a primitive state of society those cords of wood WOULD BE MONEY, and it would be a poor "simp" of a savage, indeed, who would give a year's work for nine cords of wood. The deal would be too transparent. YET THAT IS PRECISELY WHAT HAPPENS TO THE MAN WHO TAKES 3 PER CENT ON HIS MONEY.

He is "milked" or "bilked", whichever term you like to apply. Speaking plainly, he is ROBBED under conventional business methods that have been imposed on society.

Do you see what I am driving at? Suppose, living in this primitive state, you solemnly stated that seven and one-fifth cords of wood (representing a value of $9—the sum banks pay as interest for one year on $300) was all a man working 300 days could legitimately earn, and suppose you could get a man to believe that, and work for a year for those six cords of wood, would you not have (if he worked 300 days) 292 4-5 cords left, those being THE REAL FRUITS OF HIS WORK?

Think that over?

Get the FACT into your head that a dollar, roughly speaking, ought to give you the same return as one man would, working for you for an entire day, and you will at least stand emancipated from a tremendous fallacy that is taking the wealth labor creates, and giving it to a few who have not created it, and are not entitled to it.

Don't be misled by the term "money". Think of it as "labor", and then DEMAND LABOR'S WAGE.

You have, of course, seen the pictures that show labor supporting on its tired shoulders the whole structure of society, but have you realized the literal truth such pictures depict?

The dollar you work for so painfully, and that comes to you so slowly, goes almost certainly into the society hopper where the social favorites of the "clique" who exploit you spend it in an instant on the collar of a dog, or for perfumes and soaps for a favorite monkey.

This "clique", and those associated with it, can be prodigal in their expenditures, because they are giving you a fraction of what your dollar (or labor) has earned, and THEY ARE TAKING AND PROFITING BY THE ENORMOUS SURPLUS LEFT AFTER YOUR SHARE HAS BEEN GIVEN.

The mad extravagances that mark modern society are being paid for by you—by you, in blood and sweat—by you, in pleasures denied, and frugalities painfully practiced—by you, in care and worry—by you, in the life and vitality of you and yours—by you, in your painful struggle against disease and death.

Grip this pregnant fact, reader—grip it to your heart—repeat it to others.

Where do the wastrels of society get their money? Do they work for it? No! They are parasites on labor—the labor that produces all THEY enjoy.

Isn't it an anomaly? Looked at aright, isn't it crude, and raw, and WRONG?

They get it through devious and technically honest forms of law and methods of business; it comes to them through the savings banks and insurance companies, through the bonds of great corporations, through "short term notes" and through the modern fleecing pen called "Wall Street".

All they have done, all they are doing, all they are going to do, has been done, is being done and will be done with your money (labor).

This will continue unless you change—change in the habits and modes of thought that have been foisted into your mentality and which now enslave you.

The capitalist builds a paper mill which pays stockholders several hundred per cent dividends annually.

WHY CAN'T LABOR BUILD THAT MILL? WHY CAN'T LABOR TAKE THE SURPLUS ITS OWN EFFORT CREATES?

Nothing prevents labor reaping its own reward, except labor itself.

Labor must cease to regard capital as its supporter and master—labor must realize that it is the father of capital—labor must realize that all the things the world produces owe their origin TO labor, and labor must then see that IT gets what capital is now getting.

Nothing prevents labor reaping its own reward, except labor itself.

Labor must incorporate its efforts.

It must cease buying bonds, short term notes, and Wall Street speculative paper, and it must invest in COMMON STOCK of democratic corporations that take the dollars of the people and set them to work in basic industries, and then give those people back all their dollars earn, less only actual running expenses.

Labor must study the tactics of its opponent, "capital", and adopt them to its own aggrandizement. Capitalistic cliques form corporations and sell the preferred stocks and bonds, retaining the common stock and control.

Labor must form its own corporations, or support its own corporations, retaining the common stock and control.

Labor must learn that there are two ways of making money—one by working for it; the other, by making each surplus dollar work for its owner.

Labor must grasp the great fact that a dollar is in many respects a MAN.

Labor must appreciate the fact that money buys labor and that labor produces wealth.

Labor must appreciate the fact that money is simply a voucher to that wealth, and that money, of itself, has no intrinsic value.

A bag of flour and a barrel of pork would be of great value to a man on a desert island but a barrel full of gold would not.

Outside of the gifts of Nature, show me a thing in this world that labor has not produced, and that, if title were vested right, does not belong to labor.

Labor is a sleeping giant, unaware of its own terrific strength, fleeced by weaklings who govern brawn with brain; labor aimlessly fights something it doesn't understand—a phantom of the dark, as it were, that is sucking its health and happiness.

This knowledge places in Labor's hands the weapon that will bring its ghostly opponent down—the lamp that will give it light. Let labor own its own industries, and that means, eventually, all industries.

Such an ORGANIZATION of labor is utopian in a large sense—a thing that may happen after we are dead and gone; but organization is not required. Invest your labor in democratic corporations issuing common stock alone, and you have the key to a problem that has baffled the world for centuries.

If the billions now in the savings banks were invested in industries that LABOR OWNED (they are now invested in industries that CAPITAL OWNS) the millions in dividends now going to a few would be going to the many—the standards of living would be raised, and good cheer and happiness would be the birthright of all.

Labor has the intellect and brain to run its own industries. The industries of the world are run by labor now. The wastrels of the world who neither labor nor spin are spared, and can be better spared.

These things those who work with hand and brain can do:

1. They can direct investment (frozen labor) as intelligently as they direct human labor.

2. They can become investors as intelligently as capitalists can; that is, they can get investment habits and modes of thought, as capitalists do.

Roughly, it may be said that but 5 per cent of the whole population invest their funds in enterprises. Those 5 per cent, constituting one-twentieth of the whole population, GOVERN THE REMAINDER.

To get at the heart of these basic questions we must think in big, rough terms—refinements confuse.

When the bulk of the population think and act CREATIVELY, putting their surplus labor (money) into creative enterprises owned by themselves under conditions where they receive back the full creative possibilities of the labor invested, the average man will be a comfortable independent man, with money and leisure for the pleasures and refinements of life.

DISCOURSE XIV.

Labor asks for better conditions. It need not FIGHT "capital" to get them. It simply need ABANDON capital.

If it is not satisfied that it is getting what it is entitled to get from copper, or sugar, or oil, it need but turn its attention to the production of copper, or sugar, or oil, and its own corporations will support all that the capitalistic corporations had supported, and support them infinitely better.

While "capital" has filched from "labor" many natural resources, it still does not possess them all; and labor should turn to THOSE THAT ARE LEFT, which are fruitful and pregnant.

Perhaps you see the benefits of socialism, without its untried disadvantages, loom up in corporate ownership of opportunities and industries by workingmen? Does not the vision enthrall? Then the corporation will pay generous wages BECAUSE IT CAN; it will disburse generous dividends BECAUSE IT CAN. The MASS will benefit in lieu of the CLASS. This will mean that comfort and happiness will be universally distributed in lieu of being restrictively distributed, as at present.

How bring about this?

Begin yourself. Invest your labor (money) in democratic corporations that give you back all its earnings; convert your brother laborer to this viewpoint; talk it at your union gatherings; borrow the capitalistic IDEA, but in lieu of exploiting others, exploit your own opportunities.

Offer, if you must, your preferred stock and bonds to "capital" and see what capital will say or do. Whatever it does, it will certainly never BUY; create, if you must, your savings banks for capital—and see to what extent capital will appreciate your efforts. It will certainly never DEPOSIT. Offer capital all that it has offered you, and see how your offering will be SPURNED. Preach to capital all that it has preached to you, and see to what extent capital will OBSERVE IT.

DISCOURSE XV.

SAVING OR INVESTING—WHICH?

If you have considered these articles carefully thus far, you have found that they have suggested many things that you may not have previously considered with the care that they deserve.

When the captain and crew of a ship set sail from port they have a destination before them, and a specified object and gain in view when they arrive at that destination. Each member of the crew will be richer by his accumulated wages. The owners will be richer by the revenue from the freight the vessel has carried, and the vessel herself will be painted and renovated, and, if anything, better for the experience. The vessel that sails away with empty holds, without capital pledged at the end of the journey, and aimlessly into an unknown vast, will leave port loaded with gloomy forebodings, indeed.

Yes, the analogy applies closely to the ordinary human life. The average man labors for his living, and, weekly, draws drafts on his vitality and life that can not be replaced except by the equivalent of stored up labor, or money.

MAKING MONEY MAKE MONEY.

Read this editorial from the Saturday Evening Post, entitled:

"The Clerk Who Isn't Young.

"Here is a man forty-six years of age, diligent and skillful at his trade, but somewhat round-shouldered from bending over a desk for twenty-seven years. He wears spectacles, for the day-long glare of artificial light on white paper is trying to the eyes; he has a good many gray hairs, owing possibly to lack of fresh air and exercise. His corporate employer—a large concern affiliated with railroad interests—went out of business two months ago. The clerk has been industriously seeking a job ever since, but finds his gray hair, spectacles and round shoulders an insuperable bar; he might about as well go into an office bearing signs of leprosy. The answer always is:

" 'You're too old; we hire only young clerks and let them work up.'

"Meal time comes around just as though he were only twenty-one. Food is rather dear nowadays. He might move into one back room of a tenement and save a little on rent; but he hates to, because his wife is in poor health. The small savings account rapidly nears the vanishing point. It reaches that point, and he is still 'too old'. What next?

DISCOURSE XV.

"No powerful charitable organization has 'surveyed' him—partly, perhaps because he is an American, tolerably educated, keeps his clothes neatly brushed and has nothing picturesque about him.

"Of course the savings account should have been larger. He was improvident in his years of comparative affluence; sometimes took his wife to the theatre, bought a book or had a few friends to dinner. In this way—and in paying for food, rent and clothing—his eighty-five dollars a month was mostly dissipated. The trouble was exactly that he was an American, tolerably educated, and prejudiced in favor of decent living.

"He is, probably, the most pathetic figure in the country; a type of the worst-exploited and most helpless class—the city clerk. It is time to 'survey' him."

In the above we have a character sketch of the office helper, but he alone is not "the worst exploited" in the country. We have underpaid professional men, and the great army of workers who expend their capital daily in the forms of severe manual labor. Nevertheless, this man, whom for the sake of convenience, we will term John Smith, represents one of a large, universal type, and we can well dwell a little over his case. And it may be as well, reader, to ask yourself if it resembles yours in any manner or degree?

We are told that John Smith has been "exploited" and is "helpless". Now, unless the typical John Smith was told with emphasis he probably would not believe it; for men of his class and type believe that they are independent agents, and they do not believe that they are either exploited or helpless. You, reader, having read these articles, are in a position to tell him HOW he IS exploited, and WHY he IS helpless.

John Smith began to be "exploited" almost from the moment he began to realize that he was alive. It is a hundred to one that his father or mother taught him to take his pennies to the savings bank, and looked on in approval when he did so; it is a thousand to one that, beginning with his first serious magazine, and continuing with each other that he subscribed to, he was solemnly warned against "speculative" investments, and earnestly "advised" to place his money in "the savings bank", or into "approved bond investments". John Smith was simply saturated with the conventional creeds instilled into the mass of the people by and through which five per cent of the population govern the remaining ninety-five per cent.

DISCOURSE XV.

Now look at this question fairly and squarely in the light of the articles that have preceded this, if you will, but, better still, in the light of ADDITIONAL FACTS. To what does this savings habit lead? IT LEADS MILLIONS TO PRECISELY THE POSITION OCCUPIED BY JOHN SMITH. Now if it leads to that position, must it not be wrong? The fact is, it is half wrong and half right. When I adjure a young man to save I put into his mind a half truth. I should tell him TO SAVE and TO MAKE.

Benjamin Franklin was the great exponent of saving; yet, in illustrating what money does, he unconsciously used the word "make" when he said: "Money makes money, and the money that money makes, makes more money."

This is something very different from the saving creed, and the sooner men realize it the better it will be for their welfare.

In the United States great natural opportunities literally "rot" until "capital" is ready to exploit them. It is a well known fact that the "outsider" cannot touch these opportunities without the consent of Wall Street, and the control, which means that if the men who develop the opportunity link their forces with Wall Street they have to give up their birthright and sell out the men who supported them.

MAKING MONEY MAKE MONEY.

If you have a good money-making opportunity that requires capital for development and go to Wall Street, or its capitalistic associates throughout the country, to get the capital, you will get it on their terms, which are that they will take from you, in exchange for capital for development, PRACTICALLY ALL YOU HAVE.

A typical case was presented a few months ago. A man had discovered a mineral deposit in the West that is badly needed because the war has shut out importation of it. This deposit showed a value of several hundred million dollars, but the man needed half a million to begin marketing the mineral. He went to capitalists. Yes, they would take it, and that was what they meant, too. They offered to take over his property and finance it, and in return they offered him a permanent job as superintendent of the works at $150 a month!

Can you blame this man if he gives the public—the small investors—49 per cent of his property in exchange for the required capital?

Why has what we call "Wall Street" this power?

Because it controls the channels or courses through which the people's money flows, or because it controls the forces that make these channels.

DISCOURSE XV.

What is the greatest force in the world? THOUGHT. Who mould THOUGHT? The magazines and periodicals. By and through whom do these periodicals exist? Through their advertisers. The revenue from SUBSCRIBTIONS is, notoriously, not nearly sufficient to meet expenses. What is the cost of advertising? Very heavy—in some instances $6,000 a page a single insertion, and frequently from $400 to $800 a page. What sort of men can largely and consistently advertise? Capitalists, of course, or men linked to the capitalistic classes.

Let a magazine be "radical"—let it tell bald, crude truths, and what happens? Its advertising revenue falls off, and if it continues to be radical it is soon automatically and effectively "broke".

These are raw, crude facts, and if you do not happen to know of them, write the magazines—the conservative magazines—and learn what they charge for advertising space.

It is not necessary to go further into this subject. It is not necessary to go into details about the "kept" press and the many influential publications that are owned absolutely by Wall Street men, are given over unreservedly to the dissemination of the Wall Street doctrine.

So we find John Smith's thought is moulded by the power of thought as expressed in the great periodicals he reads, and we find his mentality so impregnated with the thought that he absorbs that he would scout as an enemy. and as a man that had designs on his purse, the one who would even suggest to him that his money can earn more, far more, than it earns in his savings bank or through the conservative bond house with which he does business. And this thought has colored the mentality of the entire nation, so that it is a well known fact that the projectors of an enterprise who KNOW it can pay hundreds per cent are AFRAID to publicly mention its earnings, and AFRAID to give the public securities giving those earnings, because they would be mentally classed by John Smith and his associates as "fakirs"!

We simply say this—John Smith may be right, or he may be wrong. The fact we are concerned with is this: to WHERE does this thought lead him? You have your answer in the clipping from a great magazine. It leads him inevitably to hardship and want in old age.

Ninety-five per cent of the whole population die poor.

A very large part of this 95 per cent are only a few weeks removed from actual want.

DISCOURSE XV.

The road to independence does NOT lie along the path traversed by the average man. Nothing can be plainer to the man who will simply look at things square in the face.

Five per cent of the whole population of America are men of large earnings and means —WHAT DO THEY DO?

Perhaps, if we study and follow the methods of those who succeed, in lieu of those who fail —most unfortunately, but still fail—we may get at the factors that insure success.

These 5 per cent are not patrons of the savings banks.

They are not patrons of the bond houses.

Their funds go into commercial banks—that frequently pay no interest—and their deposits in these banks are made chiefly to secure loans from them.

Not only have these men their own funds in active use in industrial enterprises, but they borrow all the funds they can and put the borrowed money in the same channel.

They saved, at the beginning, sufficient to buy a share of stock paying from 15 to 25 per cent, pledged that share at their bank and borrowed more money with which they bought other shares of stock.

They borrowed savings bank money at 5 per cent and invested it so that it produced them

20 or 25 per cent, and they repeated the operation as frequently as possible until they became wealthy.

Let us take a typical case in vivid contrast to that of John Smith, as given by George H. Cushing in the September, 1915, issue of The Illustrated World:

"H. E. Everett, of Cleveland", says Mr. Cushing, "started to work on a salary of fifty dollars a month and saved fifteen. He retired worth five million or more."

Here, then, we have a contrast. Two men begin life. John Smith is one, out of a job and in line for charity, as we have seen, at forty-six or thereabouts—and H. E. Everett, who, under the same conditions that ruled John Smith, "retired worth five million or more."

Let us examine this authentic case of Mr. Everett. Whatever else we will find, we are certain to find that his actions and policies were in direct opposition to those that guided the life of John Smith. We will take his own words:

"I saved for a year and had $180, or enough to buy two shares of stock in the Cleveland company for which I worked. It was paying dividends of more than seven per cent. When I had saved a little more, I took my stock to the bank and borrowed some money on it. With the borrowed money and my savings I had enough to pay for two shares more. My stock paid me about thirty-five dollars a year in dividends. I WAS PAYING THE BANK IN INTEREST FIVE DOLLARS PER YEAR. This, with my savings, soon paid off my loans. Then I saved more money and repeated the operation on a larger scale."

Isn't that recipe for fortune very simple? Isn't it better than the John Smith way of merely saving? Let us see how Andrew Carnegie and John D. Rockefeller got their start and kept rolling up fortunes like a moving snowball until their present colossal fortunes resulted. Both these men went into a number of investments. They distributed their business risks, so that if one failed the others made good by succeeding. Carnegie had his money invested simultaneously in iron ore, ore docks, ore carrying ships, blast furnaces, billet mills and steel mills.

Mr. Cushing, in closing his excellent article, said:

"NEVER INVEST YOUR MONEY AT ALL UNLESS YOU CAN MAKE MORE OUT OF IT THAN YOU CAN BY LOANING IT OUT AT INTEREST ON REAL ESTATE MORTGAGES OR SOMETHING OF THAT KIND."

As a matter of fact, savings bank interest, real estate and bond mortgages, and "investments" of that ilk are not to be considered by the man who wants his money to get on in the world, and pull him up with it. There are hundreds of sound propositions where money can earn 7, 10, 25 or more per cent, and into these propositions your money should go.

In other words, the secret of success in investment, as well as in life, lies in the application of that old proverb: "If you want a thing done well, do it yourself." Achieve success by doing what your commercial banker does to achieve success.

Does the banker save the money deposited with him? No! He makes it WORK. He must make it work. He realizes that his bank would "go broke", just as John Smith went broke, if he simply saved it. Like Mr. Everett, he makes the money earn more money than he paid for it. He may allow 2 per cent interest on a commercial deposit, but he takes care that he makes that money earn him 5, 6 or 7 per cent, and some of it very much more.

Now catch this point:

Make your investment in a proposition that will pay more than you can earn by lending your money on real estate mortgages or on bonds, otherwise you cannot make your dividends pay more than the interest on what you have borrowed to make the investment.

The moment a share of stock begins to pay over 5 per cent a premium is paid for it, which means that you have to pay more than par to get it, and that the money you pay for it will earn only 5 per cent or thereabouts. Therefore, to get the class of stocks necessary to follow this investing rule, you must buy before they enter the dividend paying stage, and hold them tight when they do.

Here is your recipe for success:

First—LEARN THE FACTS.

Second—Use YOUR OWN reasoning powers.

Third—Decide FOR YOURSELF.

Don't follow the advice of the average man, or walk in his conventional path. That path, as we have seen, leads to the poorhouse. When you get down to hard pan, the average man doesn't know anything worth listening to.

Burn this thought into your mind:

No one ever attains wealth from his wages alone. It is only by saving one's earnings and properly investing them that one secures a competence.

Then absorb this rule:

The mistake which most persons make is in not being ready for their luck when it comes. While they are still considering its possibilities, it is up the chimney and down in the next street. The really lucky people are those who lie in wait for their luck, and seize it and cling to it until they reap its fruits. To toy with luck, as some people do, to treat it as if it were something that could wait until tomorrow, is to court inevitable disaster.

Luck is the INTELLIGENCE TO SEE and the COURAGE TO GRASP opportunity. Nothing else. Intelligence is acquired by hard study.

Take a hundred patents out of the world, and it will be plunged back into the darkness of the middle ages. The men who seized their luck and invested in those patents when young, needed judgment and courage to back judgment, but having those qualities, they made millions and dowered the world with a gift of beneficence.

Take a hundred opportunities out of America that have been seized and capitalized, and have grown to giant proportions, and the wheels of progress will be slowed down tremendously; but, fortunately, there were men WATCHING for such opportunities, and they seized them when they came. And they became independently rich through them.

In a century a hundred patents develop—a hundred opportunities that mean the world's advancement. These are BASIC opportunities, and carry the seeds of fortune to all who perceive them aright. WATCH FOR THEM.

From these develop sub-opportunities, as the steamboat developed from the railroad train, as the telephone followed electrical invention. WATCH FOR THESE.

Watch for great natural opportunities where men uncover, or propose to uncover, nature's wealth in the form of metals, or ores, or farms, or fisheries.

Watch for great industrial opportunities. A hundred million people are now crying aloud for potash and dyes and spelter and copper and tungsten, through the dearth caused by the European war.

A few months ago tungsten mining was the most profitable branch of the mining industry in this country. Since then the price of this mineral has gone up until the industry is nearly ten times as profitable as it was, and indications are that the price will continue high permanently. Watch for such opportunities and take advantage of them when they come.

Cast out of your mind the sickly thought that you can amass wealth only by saving. SAVE to MAKE only. Set your money to work for YOU—not for another man.

MAKING MONEY MAKE MONEY.

Franklin was pretty nearly always right. Keep his words in mind: "Money makes money, and the money that money makes, makes more money."

But thinking only will not do it. You must act also.

DISCOURSE XVI.

MISAPPLIED MONEY SERVICE.

Statistics at hand for from 1904 to 1914 show that during that decade our national wealth doubled in value. In other words, during those ten years our national wealth increased an average of 10 per cent a year.

This is taking into consideration all wealth that was actively employed.

It includes business enterprises that failed, those that were moderately successful, and those that were great successes—in short, all efforts to produce wealth, from failures to the greatest successes.

The average increase on all was 10 per cent a year.

The report of the comptroller of the currency, issued at the close of 1915, shows that 11,285,834 persons in the United States had $4,997,706,013 on deposit in savings banks, an average of about $442.83 to each depositor.

A little over 11 per cent of our people are savers and leave their savings in savings banks. More than eleven out of every hundred persons, counting men, women and children, each has an average of $442.83 in a savings bank, drawing from 3 to 4 per cent interest.

This is a good showing of thrift and frugality, and the spirit shown in this saving is commendable.

This money draws 3 per cent interest, amounting to $149,931,180 a year, which is distributed among the owners of it—an average of $13.28 to each depositor.

Doesn't sound bad, does it?

But let's look at it.

The average earning of all our national wealth has been 10 per cent a year. These savings depositors get 3 per cent. Hence, on this average they are losing 7 per cent a year. In other words, they are losing $349,839,421, or an average yearly loss to each depositor of nearly $31.

That doesn't sound so good.

This money is earning an average of $499,-770,601 a year. Some of it is earning very much more. The bankers and those who borrow it of the bankers are getting the difference between the 3 per cent and the average of 10 per cent—the difference between $149,931,180 and the average of $499,770,601.

And they get that difference, you may be assured of that, or they would not pay 3 per cent for it and handle it.

DISCOURSE XVI.

The question naturally arises, why should not the owners of this money use it themselves and get all that it earns?

Can you visualize the possible profit potentiality of this amount of money if it were well invested, put into activity in well managed companies engaged in profitable industries?

Many a good company has been started on a long and profitable career with a capital of a comparatively few thousand dollars.

These days a cash capital of $100,000 will work wonders in many industries.

Were the owners of the money in savings banks to set it at work as capital in companies, they could organize and finance nearly 50,000 companies, giving each a working capital of $100,000.

Think what 50,000 such companies, engaged in various profitable industrial enterprises, would do for the owners of this money, and, incidentally, for the world.

They would increase our national wealth.

They would enlarge industrial enterprise.

They would add to the consumption of the products of other industries.

They would give employment to an army of workers.

They would turn raw resources into profitable products.

They would return large annual profits to the owners of the money.

They would increase the purchasing power of the owners of the money and of the present unemployed who would then be employed.

They would give additional products to be consumed by the additional purchasing power of the owners of the money and the workers, thereby making life more comfortable.

They would return the wealth the money creates to those who rightfully should have it, namely, its owners, and not, as now, to those who get it from the banks and use it in making multimillionaires of themselves at the expense of the owners.

They would cause a distribution of wealth among the many, giving each such a moderate amount as he could use for the comfort and happiness of himself and family.

They would not create unnecessary wealth for millionaires, for which that class has no need.

The last decade was wonderful in the addition it made to our national wealth. But the indications are that the next decade will witness a still greater increase.

About a decade ago the money ring had become so high-handed as to attract public attention. The result was twofold. Investigations were made that resulted in restrictive measures and opened the eyes of many persons to the possibilities of legitimate wealth production.

These persons set about to use the information they thus gained, and the last decade saw the establishing by the people of an uncommonly large number of companies that engaged successfully in turning raw resources into marketable wealth and in commercializing ideas and new processes for the profits of those who assisted in financing the companies.

As proof of this statement it is necessary to point only in a general way to what has been done and how done in a few lines of industry.

A decade ago Standard Oil controlled practically all of the petroleum industry. Today much of it is in the hands of other companies, through additional development, financed principally by the small investor. During this time the oil fields of California and Oklahoma have been developed largely in this way until they are the wonders of the industrial world, returning almost untold millions annually in profits to the small investors.

During the same period a long chain of profitable mines has been developed and put on production throughout the West with the money of small investors. These mines are returning profits that are fabulous in comparison with the little capital invested in them.

This period also saw the successful commercializing of the automobile and the building of that industry, until the profits in many of the companies became so large that it was found necessary to conceal them from the buying public by increasing the capital stock and declaring stock dividends. The bulk of the automobile industry has been financed by the so-called small investor.

The motion picture industry is another product of this period. This has grown so rapidly that in volume and profits it is ranked next to the steel industry and only one point removed from the oil industry, and is still growing. This has been financed in its various branches almost exclusively by the small investor.

What has been done in these big industries has been done in a proportional way in the smaller and more diversified industries. Today there is scarcely a community of any importance that has not a successfully operating company of some kind that was financed by small investors. If the community is small it has at least some members who helped furnish capital to establish a local telephone line or build an electric road that serves the community and earns profits for the shareholders.

No, all the companies organized and financed, or partly financed, during those years were not great successes. Some even failed to make good. Neither did all the babies born into the world live and grow into strong, healthy boys and girls. Neither did every store started in that time become a business success. Neither was every boy and girl who entered college graduated with honors or graduated at all. Neither did every effort in any line of human endeavor prove a wonderful success.

We all realize that every known fact is the result of a knowledge of the existence of opposites—positive and negative, we may call them. Hence, we have failures as well as successes. But this doesn't stop us doing things. Only the coward "lays down".

And the records of the last decade are wonderful—simply wonderful—in the many supreme successes in comparison with the few failures. The people are waking up. They are coming into their own. They are building for themselves, for their children, and their children's children. They are beginning to use their money to build industries for themselves to pay profits to themselves, instead of letting millionaires have the use of it for next to nothing to advance them to multimillionaires.

MAKING MONEY MAKE MONEY.

Much has been done along this line of the people using their own money. Much is being done. More will be done in the next decade than has been done in any previous similar period.

And much needs to be done to effect the complete financial liberation of our people. But the light is breaking gradually, and where there is progress there is hope.

Federal Judge Grosscup never gave utterance to a better wish for the people's welfare than when he said: "I should like to see well managed industrial corporations popularized through the ownership of their securities by great numbers of people with small means, so that savings banks will decline in popularity and their deposits dwindle."

So far 11,285,834 of our people have gone no farther along the journey than to save $4,997,-706,013 and deposit it in savings banks for others to use in making themselves rich.

In the ladder of financial success the first step is to earn, the second to save, and the third to make the savings earn for their owner. These persons have learned the first and second steps, but they will not acquire wealth until they learn to take the third step. It is in taking that step that people become rich.

DISCOURSE XVI.

In this country of boundless areas of raw wealth, of ideas, processes and opportunities almost innumerable, waiting for the magic touch of capital to convert them into marketable wealth, thereby multiplying the values tenfold, hundredfold, yes, thousandfold in the form of profits for those who furnish the money, we observe the ludicrous spectacle of 11,285,834 persons letting $4,997,706,013 lie practically idle, so far as its real earning activity being of any use to them is concerned.

This money is working. It is earning profits. But it is not working for its owners. It is not earning profits for them. They get their little 3 per cent—the crumbs that those who use the money don't care to waste time to pick up.

At this writing—the beginning of 1916—the people of Chicago have over $200,000,000 deposited in savings banks—about $100 for each man, woman and child in the city.

For the fun of it, let's see what the result would be if this $100 was at work for its owner in one of the highly successful industries.. And for this illustration we will not take one of the most successful companies—simply one of the highly successful ones.

The Postum Cereal Company is highly successful from the standpoint of profits, but it is by no means one of the most successful.

MAKING MONEY MAKE MONEY.

A hundred dollars put at work—invested—in this company in 1896, when it was organized, is now reported to have earned for its owner to the close of 1915—in nineteen years—the sum of $3,297.50 in dividends, or an average of $173.55 a year.

In addition to this, the property of the company and its earning power have increased, so that the hundred dollars is now estimated to be worth $16,800.

Here, then, the hundred dollars has produced profits and increased in value, until the two items are estimated to be equal to $20,097.50.

The other hundred dollars that lay in the savings bank those nineteen years produced $57, and today is not worth a single cent more than it was the day it was left in the bank. In fact, it is worth only about half as much, because prices have nearly doubled in that time, and if taken out of the bank now it will buy only about half as much as it would have bought when it was put into the bank. The amount that it has earned during the nineteen years is, therefore, about equal to the depreciation of its buying power. The savings bank depositor may be said to stand about where he did nineteen years ago.

We find, then, that in one instance a hundred dollars became $20,097.50, and in the other it became $157.

DISCOURSE XVI.

Had the hundred dollars been put into the original capital of the company making Sapolio, it is reported that it would have earned 600 per cent yearly, equal to $11,400 for nineteen years, and would today have grown to be worth many thousand dollars.

Had it been invested in the original shares of the Cream of Wheat Company, the information at hand shows that it would have earned as much as $1,200 some years, and, in addition, would now be worth $10,000.

Had it been a part of the $5,000 originally invested in Kellogg's Corn Flakes, the report is that it would now be reproducing itself daily. From such earning power you can readily estimate what its value is.

Had it been a part of the first capitalization of the Gillette Safety Razor Company, it would by this time have grown into shares of the par value of $52,000, drawing 7 per cent dividends, amounting to $3,640 a year.

There are hundreds and hundreds of similarly profitable companies, and thousands upon thousands of companies in which the profits on original investments are uncommonly large, but not quite as spectacular as in the specific instances mentioned.

Now don't get a wrong angle on this information. Don't think that you can invest $100 now in one of these companies and get the profits here stated. The ones who get these profits are the ones who invested in the companies at the beginning, when they were first financed, the ones who furnished the original capital. To invest in them now to get the incomes mentioned, you would have to pay the original investors many thousands of dollars for the share for which they paid a hundred dollars, or possibly less.

"It is the early bird that catches the worm."

It is the early investor who makes the big profits—the one who invests in companies that are being capitalized—new companies.

Can you imagine the economic change that would take place among the people of Chicago if they had their $200,000,000, now drawing 3 per cent in savings banks, invested in the original shares of companies like those mentioned? Can you imagine the economic change that would take place in this country if the 11,285,834 savings depositors had their $4,997,706,013 in similar companies? Can you imagine the change for the better that would take place if they had their money invested in companies even only a half, a fourth, a tenth, as good?

For instance, which would you rather have—an income of $3 a year on your $100, or an income of $173.55? Which would do you and yours the more good?

Which would you rather have—your $100 worth $100, or worth $16,800? Which would do you and yours the greater good?

You can not now get into these companies and get such profits, but there are hundreds of companies formed each year in new industries that have just as good and great possibilities. These are your opportunities, as the old companies were the opportunities of those who had the judgment and courage to see and take advantage of their opportunities when the old companies were being financed.

If you are a coward—afraid to invest in a new company—afraid to use judgment and rely and act on it—go about your investing in accordance with the science practiced by most successful men, and that is, "don't put all your eggs in one basket."

Don't put all your money into one company. Distribute it among several, or many, according to the amount you have.

Then if one should fail to make good it will matter very little to you—you had but comparatively little in it, and your other companies made good in such a large way that the loss in the one that was a failure did not amount to anything.

MAKING MONEY MAKE MONEY.

When a company is formed under favorable conditions with an honest and competent management to operate in a profitable industry with conditions favorable for large profits, you can't afford not to take some shares in it if you have money available for investment.

DISCOURSE XVII.

COURAGE AND JUDGMENT SPELL SUCCESS.

As we approach our conclusion it may be well for us to consider briefly what the lessons contained in these discourses really mean.

To understand what they mean we must understand the time and place and conditions under which they are written. This is the twentieth century, in which we find that the great nations of Europe have filled their cup—that their wealth and resources have been apportioned or distributed—that Opportunity, if it exists at all, is only for the very rich, the powerful and the influential. The poor man of lowly birth in Europe will, in ninety-nine cases out of a hundred, live and die lowly and poor; first, because opportunities within his means have vanished, and, secondly, because he is rigidly bound in a class plane that prohibits him, even if he had the opportunity, from gaining the support of those who could help him to develop it. His neighbors, friends and acquaintances are very poor; and if he has the temerity to appeal to the class above him, they will turn a deaf ear to his pleadings—the thing, if managed at all, must be managed by one of their own clique or class.

WHILE AMERICA IS RAPIDLY APPROACHING THIS CONDITION, IT IS NOT THERE YET. In Europe the limitations on opportunity have been drawn so tight that it becomes impossible for the average man to escape them; in America keen and subtle minds are drawing the loops that enslave the mentalities of millions, but those loops are not tight as yet, and it is the mission of these lessons to help not alone to loosen them if the thing is humanly possible, but to cut through them and liberate the millions from a yoke that is none the less real because it is unconscious.

So, then, "What do these lessons really mean?"

They aim to make you and millions like you SEE CLEARLY, THINK CLEARLY, and ACT RIGHTLY, to the end that, before your physical and mental powers fade, you will achieve your birthright and find the secret of financial independence behind the veil you have often looked, but did not SEE.

Where is wealth—opportunity—found in America?

The pioneer, exploring virgin territory, may find it right beneath his feet, in the form of undiscovered ore; the ranger may find it in the great forests in the form of uncut timber, or in vast deposits of coal; the observant and alert may find it in the consular reports of the United States Government, indicating, as they frequently do, where opportunity is to be found for capital and labor; the inventor may find it in a new device for doing things better; the scientist may find it in a new formula or a new process.

Opportunity, like a rare bird of plumage, is here today and gone tomorrow; this morning its song may ring at your door, and, feeling that the songster may remain, you turn over and indulge in another nap; at evening the song is faintly heard miles away, and tomorrow it is GONE. It may return, and it may not; but it is always SOMEWHERE, giving SOMEONE the one lifelong chance for aggrandizement, independence and wealth.

Opportunity may come to you direct; and if it does, seize it and be satisfied. But it may not. It may come to your fellowman a thousand miles away, and he may offer you the benefit of the treasure he has found, BY PROXY; you may SHARE in the abundance uncovered, through the device of the private corporation.

Reflect again, and you will see that the great NATURAL opportunities that our country still affords—for instance, ONE state of America is larger than the whole of the German Empire—do not originate in the great cities, and it follows necessarily that the majority of those offered you BY PROXY will be hundreds or thousands of miles away.

Through the corporate device, the prospector in Alaska or British Columbia gives you, the city dweller, the chance to share in the rich ore deposits he has uncovered after enduring incredible hardships and toil.

In a little laboratory in New York sits a man who has patiently toiled for years to do something the commercial world wanted done; he has devoted his life to the quest, and grown gray and old and enfeebled in it; finally he DISCOVERS what he has sought; it has taken the best years of his life to do this thing, but when the opportunity is capitalized YOU—young and fresh and vigorous—can share in its rewards.

"But", you object, "I can only SHARE!" All right, would you participate in it from the beginning? Would you give up all that the inventor gave up before he got this thing? Would you risk all the money the sponsors of the enterprise risked when they discovered the inventor and financed him year by year until he found the thing sought? Would you pay the patent, legal, state and other fees required to protect the invention when crystallized?

DISCOURSE XVII.

Would you step forward, when these things had been done, and put up the expenses necessary for publicity work in the financing?

You may answer, "Yes!" But be careful and see if you are quite honest with yourself and with conditions before you answer so positively; you will of course put up the money—if you have it—when you KNOW it is a SURE THING; but don't forget that those who financed this thing with time, labor and money DID NOT KNOW IT WAS A SURE THING UNTIL IT ACTUALLY PROVED ITSELF.

To thousands, the inventor—growing stooped, gray and old—was "an old crank". To thousands, those who believed in him were "a bunch of fools". To thousands, those who freely gave the money which protected the fruits of his labor were "gamblers". And to thousands, those who brought the invention through all the stages necessary to give it birth as a corporation and adequately place its opportunities before the public were simply "a bunch of wildcat promoters".

Just think how you would have acted BEFORE the event happened—BEFORE the discovery was finally MADE—before you say YOU would have DONE all that the others DID—just think.

But let us come to your main objection, which

is that you "just share", and see what force that has. Don't forget that while you only share in the opportunity, you also share in the organized effort, the organized capital and the organized ability behind it. Those things mean much to you—in fact, they mean success.

Don't forget that you "share" after the very definite risk of financing the thing to a certain known stage of success has been assumed by others, and after that risk has vanished.

Don't forget that in a case like the one we are assuming, the corporation has CRYSTALLIZED a formless thing into one of definite form—that it is ready to start on its career of COMMERCIAL success, after finishing its career of INVENTIVE success—and PARTICULARLY don't forget that it is not an old corporation with its future BEHIND it, but a new corporation with its future BEFORE it.

And, after you have carefully given these factors the importance they deserve, and which you must fully realize if you are ever going to be successful in the disposition of money, think what it means TO BE IN AT THE START.

"In at the start!" There is YOUR opportunity to make good, as the men who backed the inventor before he invented made good—as the men who paid the patent and legal fees made good—as the men who put up their own good money to bring the company into being and adequately finance it prior to its public appeal for funds made good. Here is your opportunity to show your decision and your courage as they showed theirs, and to exhibit your judgment as they exhibited theirs, IN RELATION TO THE COMMERCIAL FUTURE OF THE COMPANY.

For, remember, that is the one thing you have to consider—the commercial future. What will the people of America pay for this device, convenience or utility? What is the market, and what are the annual possibilities of that market?

And now review some of the tremendous advantages of being "in at the start" in a private corporation, under conditions where you get ALL THAT YOUR MONEY EARNS, less necessary expenses of corporate operation only.

The New York American recently gave a column of space to a recital of the case of a woman in San Francisco who, in 1882, purchased sixty shares of stock in a private corporation.

She got "in at the start" to such good effect that she was "advised" that she had purchased "a lot of worthless securities", and as she had paid only a few dollars for them she buried them in a trunk to conceal her mistake, as she considered it, and then forgot all about her certificate of stock. An alert representative of a company seeking funds met her and was told:

"I don't believe in these companies. I once bought stock for which I have never got a cent".

The representative asked to see the stock. It proved to be that of the Bell Telephone Company, and worth nearly two million dollars!

Professor Alexander Graham Bell offered to sell his telephone patents to the Western Union Telegraph Company for $60,000 "at the start", but the officers of the company said it was only a toy and had no commercial value. April 1st, 1845, Professor Morse and his associates offered to sell his telegraph invention "at the start" to the Government for $100,000, only to have the proposition dismissed by the Postmaster-General as "of too conjectural a value".

Don't you see that "at the start" neither inventor, patentees, sponsors, nor the public has anything like a clear appreciation of the value of an invention, enterprise or project?

Bell Telephone, valued by the inventor himself "at the start" at $60,000, earns over $150,000,000 annually, and SIXTY SHARES "at the start" held by the San Francisco woman referred to above, are WORTH NEARLY TWO MILLION DOLLARS.

DISCOURSE XVII.

Morse and his associates "at the start" valued their invention at $100,000, while today its system is capitalized at $220,000,000!

"At the start" of the Morse patents we can imagine one of the conservative magazines addressing "Anxious Inquirer" with $5,000 or $500 or $50 to invest, somewhat as follows.

"What is known as the Morse system is controlled by a small corporation organized recently under Maine laws, for $50,000; it is a system of transmitting words by a series of dots and dashes through an electrical instrument.

"It is said that the promoters of this device recently offered it to the Government for $100,000, and that the Postmaster-General characterized it as 'too conjectural in value to warrant purchase', and also stated that 'he was not satisfied that its revenue could be made to cover expenditures'.

"Obviously the 'investment' hardly commends itself to us, and we believe the reason why will be clear to the reader.

"We invariably recommend that people in such circumstances renounce consideration of highly speculative propositions, and place their funds in income producing railroad bonds, of which the following constitute a list drawing from 4 to 4½ per cent, suitable for investment purposes", etc., etc.

In an address delivered on his eighty-first birthday, Chauncey M. Depew, formerly president of the New York Central Lines, and United States senator, said:

"In 1887 I had an option on a sixth of the Bell Telephone for some days for $10,000. I consulted the most famous telegraphic expert in the country and he advised me to drop it. 'It is a toy and commercially a fake', he said. Had I followed my strong faith in the enterprise I would today be a hundred millionaire. I have always lost money when following the advice of experts. They are governed by their data and lack imagination, and without imagination all things not demonstrated are to them worthless".

The lawyer who organized the Bell Telephone Company and afterwards became governor of Massachusetts, refused to take shares at 10 cents each in payment of his fee of $3,000. Had he done so, his fee a few years later would have grown to $60,000,000. He was afraid to come in "at the start".

We are back at our starting question, "What do these lessons really mean?" They mean what they TEACH, and that is that "God helps those who help themselves", a principle as true in the investment field as it is in everyday life. In other words, if we wish to be successful in putting our money into opportunities offered "by proxy", WE MUST THINK AND ACT FOR OURSELVES, and not be guided by either the judgment or prejudices of others, because what passes for judgment in most things of life is really prejudice, arrived at instantaneously, WITHOUT JUDGMENT BEING CALLED IN AT ALL.

In other words, the average man will condemn a new thing, irrespective of its merits or demerits, simply because it IS new.

And again, the off-hand opinion of the average man is not worth asking for. The average man doesn't know anything outside his own little rut that is worth considering.

When we go back into commercial history we find that, almost invariably, it was the "daring" spirits that flew in the face of tradition, custom, prejudice and advice that achieved success. Sometimes, indeed, these forces of prejudice have forced success on a man, because, having got in they would not let him out; and, failing to "unload" his project on others, he was forced, by their prejudices and blindness, to carry it forward whether he would or not, as Morse carried the telegraph forward.

The general opinions of the majority of persons are worth absolutely nothing. Remember that.

In looking the great facts of life squarely in the face, remember all the time that ninety-five per cent of all the people die poor, and remember that that means that ninety-five per cent of all the people have EXHIBITED SUCH POOR JUDGMENT in regard to opportunities that came to them that they passed them up. Remember that such people ARE NOT COMPETENT, by the very nature of the case, to give you advice worth taking. Remember that they cannot succeed themselves, and they cannot make you succeed. Remember that their methods of thought are keeping them poor, and it would be a miracle if they made you rich; and particularly remember that the men who have succeeded, like Gates and others, have been the men who have acted directly contrary to the way the majority of people act. In other words, remember, that in regard to investments the MAJORITY ARE ALWAYS WRONG.

"Very well", you answer, "then I will go to the small minority made up of successful men for my advice. I will go to my banker and stock exchange broker and bond house for the counsel I need."

But again do not forget that the majority of these men have succeeded by exploiting the public of which you constitute a part, honestly enough in a legal way perhaps, but nevertheless in a way calculated to better themselves at your disadvantage.

The banker wants your money in his bank. He lives by that fact, and, knowingly or unknowingly, he is hardly in the FRAME OF MIND that will lead him to advise you to take it out. The stock exchange broker wants your money for SPECULATION, and the bond house wants it in BONDS.

So you see that the men who handle money successfully are the ones who gain by the exploitation of men such as you, either by getting your money at a low rate and investing it at a high rate, and taking the difference for themselves, or by taking a fixed percentage of it whether you win or lose.

And don't forget that in Wall Street particularly and emphatically the BIG MAJORITY ARE ALWAYS WRONG. Financiers sell out when the public are buying, and buy back when the public are selling out. That's how they make THEIR money—flying in the face of tradition, custom, prejudice and advice.

If, therefore, these lessons have taught you nothing else than the value of DISTRUSTING average advice, and the value of DISTRUSTING average ways, ideas, customs and prejudices, they will have performed an enormous good and put you on the highway to success.

You know what a great thing PERSONALITY is in the affairs of life—how it makes a man stand out as "different". There is a personality of self, and a personality of money. Like the magnetic successful man, your money must act differently than the majority of money hoards, or it will remain on the dead level of mediocrity, earning a "living" interest and no more.

To get this "money personality" your dollars must ACT differently, because YOU THINK differently. Your first step towards profit in investing is to get the facts and act on those facts, and not to alter your action or determination based on those facts until someone CAN SHOW YOU that in your chain of calculations you have omitted some vital fact that makes your conclusion worthless.

Remember that after you have studied an investment, hardly anyone has studied it like you have; consequently, hardly anyone is as competent to form as accurate judgment about it as you are. Therefore, act by facts and stand by facts, because facts rule the world and facts make an enterprise successful—not blind prejudice or unreasoning condemnation.

DISCOURSE XVII.

First, learn to JUDGE. Secondly, learn to STAND BY your judgment. Thirdly, learn to ACT on your judgment. The sum of these things will make your money EARN—earn what it is entitled to—not what others CLAIM it is entitled to.

Money is simply a TOOL. To produce, it must be USED. If you cannot use it, there are others who CAN. When you know WHERE and HOW and by WHOM money can be advantageously employed, learn the art of LETTING IT GO TO WORK just as financiers and other men who make money do.

The man who finds it hard to get money is the one who grips it so hard when he gets a little of it that it cannot work. The man who finds it easy to get money is the man who handles it easily and gives it plenty of freedom to work. Free your mind, therefore, of that intense sense of POSSESSION of money that comes down subconsciously from old uncivilized times when man had to protect his hoard from rapine and plunder. Learn the facts and use judgment. Then put your dollars freely and quickly into the hands of other men, honest and conscientious men, who, by special proximity to opportunity, can make it earn for you what you cannot.

MAKING MONEY MAKE MONEY.

Here you will find the secret of financial success—doing fearlessly, on sound judgment, what the other fellow is afraid to do at all.

DISCOURSE XVIII.

ARE YOU A COWARD?

Are you a coward?

Rather an impertinent question, you suggest?

Yes, on its face it is. Also a rather serious one. It usually has a tendency to lead to unpleasant consequences.

All of us remember that in our school days the suggestion that a boy was a coward meant fight, and Dewey style, at that—hit first and talk afterwards. And most boys never grow away from that notion.

But there are proper ways to consider every unpleasant subject, and it is good for us to do so, now and then—to take an inventory of ourselves, as it were, by asking ourselves and one another some of these unpleasant and seemingly impertinent questions. It stimulates thought, and thought is good for us.

Therefore, I ask, ARE YOU A COWARD?

And right here let us bear in mind that there are two classes of cowards—physical and mental. Also that I am not referring to a physical coward. In fact, I incline to the opinion that in most instances physical cowardice is a virtue. Usually the one who so far forgets himself as a man, that the question of cowardice in resenting him may arise, is unworthy the attention of intelligent and really courageous men.

The mental coward holds a different position. He is found in all walks of life, and his cowardice assumes many forms and modes of expression.

Mental cowardice consists either of failing to do one's imperative and well defined duty in a course of action already established, or of failing to take such part as one can in the initiation of a course of action that ordinary intelligence dictates should be taken for the accomplishment of the greatest good.

Mental cowards are a menace to themselves and humanity, and frequently they work irreparable injury.

No one will deny that Benedict Arnold was a mental coward. His duty was clear. Instead of performing it, he added traitorousness to cowardice and sold his country.

James Buchanan's duty was clear when he was in the presidential chair. Failing to perform it, he let his country drift without protest into the throes of a death struggle.

DISCOURSE XVIII.

How admirably do not the mentally courageous stand out in comparison. Think of Washington and Lincoln and Grant and Dewey, and realize into what insignificant ashes such figures as Arnold and Buchanan turn. The vision stimulates emulation.

What is true in community affairs is usually true in personal matters. Those who are unfortunately situated in regard to material things are usually victims of their mental cowardice.

It follows, as a corollary, that, given the same intelligence, the person who is not fortunately situated in material things is a mental coward.

Now, then, are YOU a mental coward?

If you have reached that age at which courageous men usually have acquired a reasonable competency, or more, and you have not done so, is it not time for you to go over the account with yourself and see what you have permitted to be charged against you on the debit side?

And my observation leads me to remark—and this is about the place to do it—that there is no neutral ground in this field of cowardice and courage. You must be on one side or the other. You can not be a mixture of both. Therefore, if you are not courageous in your business affairs, if your material circumstances have not reached the stage to entitle you to be enrolled among those brave souls, those courageous knights who bear aloft the banner of industrial and financial success, you are a coward, and you are a coward whether or not you are willing to admit it.

If you are a mental coward—if you are a business afraid—you are your own worst enemy, and you should set about at once to become friendly with yourself. If you should do this—become acquainted with yourself on a friendly basis—it may be that you will soon find yourself growing into a pretty good fellow, competent for honorable courageous activity. It is rarely too late to do good—too late to improve.

Don't be a mental coward. Cowards never get anywhere.

The men who pushed forward on the pioneer lines in this country were not cowards. The men who built the great railroads into the wilderness in anticipation of reward from industries yet to be were not cowards. The men who built the cities, who established the great industrial enterprises, who founded the gigantic financial institutions were not cowards. And the men who could not participate directly in the great work of these productive activities, but who entrusted their money as investments with the men who were on the firing line of these affairs, were not cowards. They were courageous titans who saw clearly, judged wisely and acted well. All were rewarded according to what they did. The rich families of America today are the result of this courage. These families are now furnishing much of the financial blood in the body of still greater American industrial progress.

These hundreds of thousands of courageous builders did not always win. They did not always see the end clearly. Now and then they failed in an enterprise. But did that stop them? Did they lie down and wail about their luck? No. Failure but intensified their passion for success. Mistakes but taught them to avoid making them again. And with their wider experience and keener vision they redoubled their efforts and won in a greater measure than if they had not made mistakes.

They were not afraid. They were not cowards.

Every big industrial enterprise of today had its beginning in the courageous activity of the one who conceived its possibilities and strove to make the conception real. These tremendous affairs of today did not fall, like the manna of the Israelites, in finished form into the hands of their founders. No, they are the result of courageous activity, of well planned and competently executed enterprise.

And the founders of these gigantic industries and businesses could not have done what they did had there not been others of equal courage who saw keenly and acted courageously in investing money with which to build into auctalities the conceptions of the founders.

From an idea in the brain of Stephenson to the present network of railways that covers the land surface of the globe, bringing practically every little back-country hamlet in touch with the world, is a long stretch. It required courage and money to go that distance.

From Fulton's little steamboat on the Hudron river to the craft that circle the earth and ply the inland waters is a mighty step. It was not taken by cowards, either in doing or in investing.

From Edison groping in a little laboratory to the world illumined and its countless wheels turning by a new power is an industrial span too great for the comprehension of the ordinary mind. It required courage to accomplish all this.

From puttering with an idea in a country blacksmith shop to supplying the world with its harvesting machinery is another step that would cause cowards to quake were they asked to help take it.

From an idea involving the transmission of thought to the actual instantaneous delivery of a message on the opposite side of the globe, involving the building of an industrial enterprise employing tens of thousands of workers and hundreds of millions of capital, was a step that required courage. It was no coward's work.

And so we could continue to entertain ourselves by reviewing many other big lines of activity that required courageous action to establish, and that have brought rewards commensurate with the courage manifested.

To build our cities and establish the lines of business conducted in them required the keen foresight of courageous souls. This has been the work of many workers. Some conceived the ideas, some planned boldly, others invested courageously, and others executed wisely. All were courageous. All took a chance. All were optimists. All were rewarded according to their activity. And the world received the benefit of more comforts and greater conveniences.

Those who did these things were the few—the courageous.

The others? Oh, they were the cowards, who

stood by cursing their "luck" and envying the others.

That's all.

Are you a coward?

When your chance comes, are you afraid?

Do you let your vision become blurred by the thought that possibly if you take a chance you may lose a few dollars?

That thought is the whipping post to which most persons are lashed, and it is hard for them to break away. They are, in fact, afraid to break away from it. They cling to it as the savages, in their ignorance, cling to a fetish. They are cowards.

Every business venture, whether by oneself or with others in corporate form, involves a chance. If the venture is well founded and well organized and well managed, the chance is so small that it is not worth considering. Were we not to take that chance, we would not have any business enterprises. The world would go back to barbarism and then stand still.

The courageous take that chance. The cowards do not.

The courageous may lose once in a while, but they win so often that they become rich and the bearers aloft of our civilization.

The cowards neither win nor lose. They

stand still. They stagnate. They go down to death in a humble cottage or the poorhouse.

Who wants to be a coward?

Ask yourself sincerely, friend, if you are one.

If you find you are, won't you take my solicitous advice that you should try to reform?

"America! Another name for Opportunity," as Emerson said, has more opportunities today than ever before. They are waiting on every hand. Select yours. There is no reason why you should go down to death in a humble cottage or in the poorhouse. There is wealth enough for all, waiting to be developed and distributed.

DISCOURSE XIX.

BUILDING FORTUNES.

In the written and unwritten industrial and financial history of America are hundreds of thousands of chapters, each devoted to a man or a clique of men, showing how the courageous have won fortunes.

It will be interesting to refer briefly to a few of these in different lines of activity. What is true of a few is true of the many, the lesser circumstances only being altered. The instances given may be taken as types of the many.

There are two types of men and women who accumulate money—the first SAVE, and the second SPEND.

It may seem a strange statement that men make money by spending it, yet it will be seen that it is as true as is the fact that other men make money by saving it.

A man has a business, position or "job" which gives him a stated sum monthly. His entire ingenuity and effort is centered on reducing his running expenses to the end that each month he will have a larger surplus to put into the savings bank. In pursuit of this aim he will lead very often a narrow, constricted life, depriving himself, through motives of frugality, of different kinds of pleasures.

The motto that governs such persons is "live within your income."

On examination it will usually be found that persons of this type come from the continent of Europe, and in their conduct are governed by European traditions and customs. A native of France, for illustration, is, by habit, circumstance and environment, A SAVER, putting his little hoards, periodically, into French Rentes, or into the bonds recommended to his attention by the great French banks. The French have been rightly termed a "nation of investors."

Those of the second type are either native Americans, or the descendants of European parents. They have outlived the traditions of the countries that gave their fathers birth, and are impregnated with the American spirit that gets money by spending money.

They stand out in marked and curious contrast to the Europeans who have been whisked, as it were, from a land of frugality to one of opportunity—from a land that at best could hold out to them only freedom from dependency in old age, to a land that could promise them independence or fortune, provided they spent freely, saved but little, and invested or speculated much.

The European suit of clothes is carefully brushed and mended and worn threadbare before it is discarded; the American suit is discarded the moment it begins to look a little worn and shabby. European offices are furnished without regard for appearances; American offices are furnished with all regard for appearances. The European with a thousand dollars puts it into the savings bank, or into Government bonds; the American is very apt to put it into some fast growing business enterprise.

Each type, really representing a nation, is making money in its own way; and when the thing is analyzed, in the best way consistent with circumstances. Europe has its opportunities behind her; America's opportunities are all before her. The European has no field to speculate in, while in America it is somewhat difficult to do anything but speculate. "The man who is a bear on the future of this country", said the late J. P. Morgan, "will go broke." So Americans feel, and it must be said that their faith is justified by results; they are optimists, and optimists let go a dollar to make two—or three, or four.

Optimists make a good impression by dressing well. By virtue of that impression they make friends and acquaintances that help them make more money. They give a good business impression by furnishing luxuriously appointed offices, and the investment pays most handsomely in the increased business gotten as a consequence. The twentieth century American is a SPENDER, and he is making his money by SPENDING. No fact stands out more clearly on observation.

When Henry Ford began to work on the universal car that has made the automobile famous, A. Y. Malcomson, a coal dealer, SPENT some $7,000 with him. Malcomson told his bookkeeper about the idea, and he in turn was interested enough to spend $1,400 that he had, and to put in a note for $1,000 that he had not, but which he hoped to have—see the distinctively American idea of spending what was in hand, and borrowing for what was not? Couzens in turn went to his sister, who had saved up $100 by slow degrees, and got her to spend the entire sum for a little interest in the matter which they arranged to set apart for her.

Mr. Malcomson, it seems, still had the "spending itch", because, unable to buy more himself, he did the next best thing and explained the project to a Mr. J. S. Grav, who put in

$10,000 after Malcomson had guaranteed him against loss—see the workings of the cautious European mind?

Two brothers—Dodge Brothers—who were running a bicycle sales and repair shop, then scraped up and spent some $10,000 with Ford, and John W. Anderson and Horace H. Rackham, a struggling pair of lawyers, spent $5,000 in the same direction.

History records what happened to these persons who SPENT instead of SAVED.

Miss Couzens, for her initial $100 spent, has taken $47,000 from the Ford Motor Company in cash dividends, and still has $50,000 worth of stock.

Dodge Brothers, from the original investment of $10,000, received $5,000,000 in cash, in addition to which they now hold $5,200,000 in stock.

The little law firm of Anderson and Rackham, who scraped up and spent $5,000, saw its partners dowered with $2,500,000 each, while each now holds a bit more than that amount in stock.

And the future profits of these persons now loom much greater than those in the past. The company is reported to be making and selling more automobiles than ever before, and to this business it is proposed to add an assuredly profitable tractor manufacturing and selling business.

So we see how it sometimes pays to spend money rather than save it; and from it we can deduct the conclusion that while the savers get along very well in Europe, which cannot offer opportunities, they do not get along nearly so well in America, which can.

The average American regards money as a TOOL that he uses with which to make more money; and it is a curious paradox that, through this viewpoint, the more he spends the more he makes. If one reads the life history of Carnegie, or, for that matter, any of the kings of fortune that America has produced, one is at once struck by the fact that their lives were a continuous outlay. And frequently we witness, year after year, the spectacle of successful men, very nearly "broke", reaching with their own money, the money they can borrow, and the money of friends and acquaintances, after the thing that looks good to them.

At their birth, all things looked like things of speculation and risk. The European type of mind will have none of them—it clings to its savings banks and its government bonds. The American type of mind, however, measures the risk, measures the profit, jumps the gap by judgment, ACCEPTS them, spends WITH them, and WINS with them, as did the men who backed Ford, and who, with him, through the American temperament that made them spend what little they had to get more—vastly more—were flung on gold thrones.

It is men of this type that have made America. It is men of this type that will build her still greater.

January 1, 1914, the regular legal reserve life insurance companies of America held assets of the value of $4,658,696,337, received in premiums $714,809,356, and enjoyed a total income of $469,588,123. If you can grasp what these stupdendous sums really mean and represent, you have a better imagination and calculating sense than have most persons.

Be that as it may, we know, at least, that the great life insurance companies of today are towers of financial strength, and we know that their business, BUILT ON SPECULATION AND CHANCE, is the most certain of any business in the world. That's a curious fact when you come to think of it, isn't it? But it's so.

But it was not always so. As a matter of fact, the business of life insurance did not exist prior to 1583. In that year a policy for 383 pounds, 6 shillings and 8 pence was written on the life of William Gibbons, sixteen underwriters signing it, each severally for his own share, the premium charged being 8 per cent of the amount called for.

It is interesting to note, in these days of highly developed insurance, that the age of the insured was not referred to, nor, we are informed, was it considered material! The premium, in a very large sense, was guessed at; in other words, the transaction represented a gamble.

It is interesting to note, also, that this initial transaction, from which was to spring our gigantic life insurance companies of today, controlling and disbursing billions of dollars, ended in loss, Mr. Gibbons dying on the 29th of May, 1584.

Back in the 17th century, a few isolated instances of similar contracts are found, and in 1720 the British Parliament chartered the Royal Exchange and the London Assurance Company, and the following year witnessed an organized effort to write policies of life insurance throughout England.

The business in those days was, as may be imagined, wrapped in the mists of uncertainty and doubt, and even to the well informed it appeared most hazardous and speculative, representing a class of enterprise that could hardly be classed as an "investment", but coming under the category of the speculative, or even "wild-cat", class.

It can, therefore, be imagined that, in 1875, when the Prudential Insurance Company of America was selling its shares of stock that it had some very real difficulties to meet, and that those who bought had to be coaxed, bullied or cajoled into buying; and, further, that many who were so cajoled bitterly regretted the step on reflection, and fought to escape the outlay they had obligated themselves to make.

Under such conditions of time, place and circumstance, one William Robatham bought twenty shares of Prudential stock on the thirteenth of October, 1875, paying $200, or 20 per cent, on account of the purchase price thereof. Robatham must have been fast on the heels of opportunity when he made this deal, because, according to the affidavit of Forrest F. Dryden, made under subsequent legal proceedings on the 10th of November, 1902, "the remaining $800 due on said stock was subsequently paid for in cash by dividends applied to the balance due on said stock." Robatham, it seems, had contracted to take sixty shares in all, and, aided by cash dividends applied by the company towards payment, he settled for the balance of his shares on the 17th of July, 1879.

"Said William Robatham", testified Forrest F. Dryden, "subsequently received from said company 913 97/100 shares in stock dividends, declared from time to time on his said holdings, said 913 97/100 shares having a par value of $45,698.50. Thus the said Robatham has owned in the past 973 97/100 shares, for which he paid out in cash the sum of $2,200. He is now the owner of 600 shares. Therefore, he has sold 373 97/100 shares, which if sold at an average price of $275 a share, which I believe to be far below the price he has realized therefrom, netted him $102,841.75. During the time he has owned stock in the company he has received in the way of dividends in cash a sum amounting to $46,521.85, and he still owns 600 shares of a par value of $30,000, which at $600 a share—the price offered by the Fildelity Trust Company to Prudential stockholders—would net him $180,000; so that should he accept the offer of the Trust Company he would have received altogether as a return for his investment of $2,200 the sum of $329,363.60."

An investment of $2,200 that produces an average yearly profit of $12,117.17, or over 550 per cent, is quite industrious, and a little out of the common, to be sure. It looks big, and to the one who has not learned to exercise his judgment and initiative beyond accepting 3 per cent from savings banks, or from 5 to 6 per cent on bonds, it looks like the impossible. But in this instance the facts and figures were given under oath and under conditions where the truth of the statements could be ascertained by cross-examination.

Andrew Carnegie was born in a humble little cottage in "the old country". His father, dissatisfied with conditions that ruled at home in his trade of weaving, emigrated to America in 1848, and the son began his business life at about the age of fourteen, firing a furnace and running a bobbin engine.

From eighteen to twenty-five he became noted for his proclivity for putting his savings into outside enterprises, and was interested even then, we are told, in a score or more of promising projects, through which, combined with other activities, he secured capital sufficient to enter business for himself.

At this stage a friend became involved in a dispute with his business partner, and both came to him with their difficulties, the outcome being that he became interested in their business, in which he subsequently acquired a substantial interest by "trading in" the Cyclops Mill and a lump sum of $50,000 in return for a little less than half of the shares of a new company, of which Andrew Kloman was to be manager, termed the Union Iron Mills Company, organized with a capital of half a million dollars.

This time it is interesting to note that when the venture above outlined had been made, he felt keenly disappointed, writing his friend Miller a couple of years later, saying:

"I knew you had previously been wronged, and felt that you could not forget it. I did what I could at the time to redress the wrong, and went into the most hazardous enterprise I ever expect to have any connection with again, the building of a rival mill."

J. H. Bridge, who chronicled this incident, has said: "It was in this strange guise (referring to the business dispute that first brought the Kloman brothers to the attention of Carnegie) that Dame Fortune, having already gently tapped several times at Carnegie's door, now began a regular tattoo; but so busy was he with his little schemes that many years passed before he realized the meaning of the noise."

Mr. Bridge further states, in commenting on his remarkable letter to Mr. Miller:

"And so, regarding it as a 'most hazardous enterprise', Andrew Carnegie found himself fortuitously and complainingly thrust upon a road which was to lead him to a fortune of $250,000,000."

Michelet once wrote, "Woman is a miracle of divine contradictions"; and when we remember that Fortune is typified in song and story as a dame, we begin to understand what men have termed "Carnegie Luck".

In this instance the lady seems to have taken a stubbornly perverse interest in Andrew, taking his repulses as the signal to shower him with additional gifts. We learn, for instance, that, despite his earlier successes, he adopted for his guidance the little investment epigram, "Pioneering doesn't pay", and in the spirit of that phrase opposed the erection of the slabbing-mills at Homestead, which later paid their cost within two years. In the same manner he opposed the acquisition of a half interest in the stock of the Oliver Mining Company, conditioned on a loan of half a million dollars, secured by a mortgage on the ore properties, to be spent in development work, arranged in such a way that the Carnegie ore interest would really not cost anything.

Writing about this at the time (1892), Mr. Carnegie said:

"Oliver's ore bargain is just like him—nothing in it. If there is any department of business which offers no inducement, it is ore. It never has been very profitable, and the Massaba is not the last great deposit that Lake Superior has to reveal.''

Mr. Frick, however, made the bargain with Mr. Oliver—at the loss of Mr. Carnegie's friendship, the latter writing after the deal was made:

''The Oliver bargain I do not regard as very valuable. You will find that this ore venture, like all our other ventures in ore, will result in more trouble and less profit than almost any branch of our business. If any of our brilliant and talented young partners have more time, or attention, than is required for their present duties, they will find sources of much greater profit right at home. I hope you will make a note of this prophecy.''

Those properties, it should be noted, combined with others, the acquisition of which Mr. Carnegie again opposed, gave the Carnegie-Oliver interests their impregnable position in the iron industry of the country. Mr. Bridge, in commenting on ''this great gift which Andrew Carnegie reluctantly allowed Mr. Frick to accept'', says:

''Andrew Carnegie often says that Fortune timidly knocks at every man's door at least once during his lifetime. The statement is too modest to fit his case; for Fortune has repeatedly battered down the barricades with which he has tried to exclude her. Nor has she been scared away by the inscription above the Carnegie threshold, 'Pioneering doesn't pay'."

In the whole of Carnegie's career, in fact, we find a peculiar reversal of usual conditions. Ninety-five per cent of the people die poor, and these end in poverty through treading the path that the unsuccessful are treading, and accepting the advice and counsel of men who cannot better themselves, let alone others. Carnegie, in his more mature years, tried to tread the path of mediocrity, but was literally forced out of it by those associated with him; fortune was thrust into his hands against his will and judgment, until we see him at the end in possession of a business worth five hundred millions of dollars—"the total cash value of the business to which Kloman's little forge had grown in forty years".

Today little enterprises, destined to form the giant oaks of commerce and business, are sprouting throughout the land. The heritage they will come to is for you to share, if you "pioneer" as Carnegie did in his earlier years, thus getting the money to make his BIG financial start; and provided that when the big swing really begins, you still keep in mind the big important fact that when judgment and brains back Opportunity pioneering DOES pay.

The story goes in financial circles that a little over twenty years ago Charles W. Post, broken in health, was taking treatment at a Battle Creek, Michigan, sanitarium noted for dietetics.

They fed him their health foods, and he got well.

This gave him an idea: If these foods helped to make SICK people WELL, why should they not keep WELL people WELL? If they would, why shouldn't well people want to eat them? If well people would want to eat them, why shouldn't there be a lot of money in making and selling them?

Asking investigating questions almost invariably leads to action, to courageous enterprise. So it did in this instance.

Mr. Post invented some health foods of his own, and, scraping together $750, in January, 1895, began manufacturing them in a little barn in Battle Creek.

In Postum, Mr. Post had a beverage to which no normal palate would take kindly, and that consequently it could get a place in the menu only through psychological suggestion; in other words, it would have to be forced politely down people's throats. If this could be done, it had a world-wide field. If this could be done without too great an expense, it would be a big moneymaker.

Mr. Post took a big chance to win by clever advertising. He gave the people in a little nicer form the beverage that the pioneers used in place of coffee when they were too poor to buy coffee, and by talking cleverly to them about it, made them believe it was a privilege to have the opportunity to get his beverage.

The history of Mr. Post's venture is interesting in a business way. So far as Postum is concerned, it must be admitted that he started with a bad idea—chances against him too long. He had the ability to overcome those chances, and because his product was adapted to nation-wide consumption he made a great financial success. It illustrates forcibly that if you have a meritorious article for common consumption—an article that no one else has—and can get it before all the people, there is practically no limit to the size of the fortune it will build for you.

As Mr. Armour, founder of Armour & Co., the world-renowned packing house, said to a young friend who asked his advice about going into business: "Make and sell things that are 'et' up!"

Mr. Post started his business with $750 in a little barn. The following year he organized a company with a capitalization of $5,000,000. Information from financial circles is to the effect that he had the usual difficulty to secure capital. Those who have inside information say the business can not be bought now for $20,000,000. It has paid and is paying fabulous dividends.

The business was started in a little barn. Today is occupies over twenty large buildings filled with power-driven machinery.

In a recent legal tangle in connection with the settling of Mr. Post's estate it was made of record that it was worth $33,000,000, of which only a part is his interest in the cereal company. Here a dollar of original capital grew into $44,000 in twenty years. Making and selling things to eat made him wealthy, and many others with him who had the opportunity and the judgment to accept it to join him.

To build a fortune surely and steadily, "Make and sell things that are 'et' up".

This quotation is applied figuratively, of course. A monopoly, or what approaches a monopoly, in any article that is used, consumed or worn out by all the people, and bought again and again, carrying a good or reasonable profit, is a sure source to fortune when in the hands of competent and honest management.

If you do not want to seek fortune in nature's raw resources, tie your wagon to the star of such a product, under such conditions, and it will roll you along on the road to fortune, and you can't stop your progress without selling your seat to someone else.

The Reo Motor Car Company was organized at Lansing, Mich., in 1904, with a capitalization of $500,000.

It had the usual difficulty of new companies in raising capital with which to begin operations.

"Billy" Grove, the then genial clerk of the Downey House at that place, had faith in the enterprise and invested his savings of $1,000.

Now he is manager of the Downey House.

At the beginning of 1916, when the Reo stockholders met and decided to increase the capitalization of the company to $10,000,000, at the same time voting a 100 per cent stock dividend, Billy sat down and figured up how much his thousand-dollar investment had developed into in the eleven years since the inception of Reo. He found that it now amounted to $119,050.

In order to understand this tremendous increase one must remember that the capitalization of the Reo Motor Car Company was increased from $500,000 to one million, later to four millions, and now to ten millions; and that beside the stock dividends declared at those various times, there has been something like 1,500 per cent in cash dividends disbursed among the Reo shareholders.

Billy Grove's original thousand dollars' worth of stock has developed into twenty-four hundred shares. This, at the present market value, plus the cash dividends he has received, gives him a net earning on his original thousand of more than $118,000.

"And best of all", said Donald E. Bates, secretary and treasurer of the company, "is the fact that Billy Grove's story is precisely the story of a great many other Lansing people who had confidence in the men who organized the Reo company, and whose confidence has been justified and so handsomely rewarded."

This is another forceful illustration of the advantage those have who secure shares from the original capitalization of a company. Should Billy Grove desire to do so, he could now "cash in" by selling his 2,400 shares, of which he has paid for only 100, having received the other 2,300 as stock dividends. In the meantime, he has received cash dividends to return to him more than the $1,000 he paid for his shares, together with good interest on the money during these years.

It is nearly half a century sinee B. F. Lyon decided to build a book paper mill at Kalamazoo, Michigan. Men who were asked to join the enterprise scouted it as a foolish venture.

"Why make paper in Kalamazoo?" they asked.

Nobody had ever made it before in that region. There really seemed no particular reason for starting such a venture in Kalamazoo, except that Mr. Lyon happened to live there.

Mr. Lyon experienced, therefore, quite some difficulty in getting people interested in this venture, but some $80,000 was ultimately scraped together by the small contributions of patriotic and venturesome local business men. It took hard persuasion, even at that, and one of the bankers, who had been dragged into the proposition, sold out his stock at 50 cents on the dollar, and many of the original subscribers followed his example.

The management, however, secure in the belief that it was on the right track, went into the specialty market and engaged experienced paper makers, like S. A. Gibson, a master mechanic from Massachusetts; Noah Bryant, who had gained a wide experience in English paper mills, and others, who brought business and technical capacity to bear on the problem.

As a result, the mill came into the dividend paying stage, and to the great consternation of the banker who had sold out at 50 cents on the dollar, and those who had sold out with him, the average dividend return to stockholders was over 40 per cent annually.

In 1887 Messrs. Bardeen and Bryant, with three others, retired from the original mill and set up as an independent concern; this time local investors knew the industry was profitable, because they had the example of the now prosperous paper business before them. "But", they argued, "this new mill will never get a start; the old mill will put it down and out."

However, the new concern got a little capital and began with one machine. It earned good money and put in other machines out of the profits it made, because from the viewpoint of the majority of the community it was still doomed to failure when the older business really got after it. These prophets of disaster were, however, considerably astonished when dividends ranging from 20 to 60 per cent respectively began to be paid.

Mr. Bryant was still unsatisfied, however.

He felt that with greater manufacturing facilities much more money could be made; and he had, furthermore, all the pride of a workman in his craft, and wanted to see a factory and business grow up in Kalamazoo that would stand as an example to the paper makers of the country, and prove a monument to the business enterprise that originated it.

Charles B. Hayes and several others who had been associated with the former successes now joined forces with Mr. Bryant and organized a company with a capital of $125,000. This, gauged by manufacturing standards in the paper line, was an exceedingly modest beginning. Nevertheless, those connected with it realized that they had a good thing, and, putting back profits and dividends into upbuilding, they soon had a very large concern with five mills, containing ten paper machines, thirty coating machines, and capitalized at $3,500,000.

For a long time this latter concern paid dividends of 5 per cent a month. About eight years ago it declared a stock dividend of 550 per cent, each holder of one share receiving, without any outlay, five and a half new shares. Even after this readjustment the shares sold at three and a half times their face value! Several years accumulated profits were distributed in the form of a hundred per cent stock dividend, each shareholder getting one new share again, gratis, for each old share.

That was making money.

If you had invested $1,000 in this business when it began, you would have received for many years 5 per cent a month, or six hundred dollars a year in cash dividends; today, without any additional investment, the stock you would hold would be of the face value of $13,000, and have a market value of over $20,000.

DISCOURSE XX.

CONCLUSION.

"It has been well observed that we should treat futurity as an aged friend from whom we expect a rich legacy." So said Colton.

We are looking towards the future, as captains and crew look towards the distant port for which they are sailing where the rich cargo carried will be turned into money, where the owners will get the profit on their investment and enterprise, where the captain will get the reward for his skill, and where the members of the crew, in their wages, will get paid for their labor.

Observe that under the conditions of a normal voyage, the owners will get the greater share, as is right, and observe, also, that this share comes to them as a reward for their INVESTMENT and ENTERPRISE.

Now, as the heart, soul and title of this series of articles is the world "investment", let us examine into its meaning. Ordinarily the words "investment" and "speculation" are considered as opposed in meaning; yet, when we turn to that great authority, the New Standard Dictionary, we find the latter word defined as follows:

"SPECULATION: to make a purchase or INVESTMENT that involves a risk of loss, but also offers a chance of considerable profit."

Note carefully that this authoritative work makes "investment" and "speculation" synonymous; in other words, in this definition they both stand for about the same thing and the same act.

And rightly. Money in the savings bank at 3 or 4 per cent is not investment—it is being SAVED, and money in bonds at a similar rate is also being SAVED.

YOU ARE NOT USING THE PRINCIPAL —others are.

Almost everything we do is both a speculation and an investment. We speculate a dollar on a theatre ticket in the EXPECTATION that we will see a good show. The show itself will prove if we have lost or won.

Speculation and investment BOTH involve risk, and it can only be escaped by SAVING money instead of investing it. Every man starting in business assumes a business risk. The Standard defines business as "a commercial enterprise", and then defines enterprise as "a venture".

DISCOURSE XX.

Savings banks, life insurance companies, public service corporations, railroads, etc., all begin business as a "venture", "undertaking", "scheme", or "attempt to perform".

In another sense, the word enterprise is defined as "boldness, energy, and invention exhibited in practical affairs, especially in business—energetic and progressive."

In the antonyms of "enterprise" we find "unenterprising, dull, inactive, slow, stupid, timid."

Practically every investment is based on business, which means enterprise, which in turn means boldness, energy and invention in business affairs; and when we turn to the opposite condition, we find terms that precisely describe money that (so far as the owner is concerned) is allowed to accumulate instead of work (the banks see that it works for THEM—be sure of that). In other words, this money is inactive, dull, slow, stupid and timid.

Our doubts are traitors,
And make us lose the good we oft might win,
By fearing to attempt.—Shakespeare.

We find these latter qualities hiding under the exceedingly handy and comforting word, "conservative"; and we hear a good deal from men we know to be "bold, energetic and progressive" in their business affairs, about the advisability of making "conservative investments''. Indeed, one of our greatest multi-millionaires, when interviewed, always delivers a very instructive homily on the virtue of saving.

This man takes the money of timid owners that they have put into life insurance companies and banking institutions, and, by enterprise and invention in practical business affairs, makes it work exceedingly hard for HIM, as witness his stupendous fortune which a hundred thousand men could never have ''saved'' in the course of their aggregate lives.

We find, in short, these men PREACHING in terms that would be inconsistent, to say the least, if they were used as symbols to represent their everyday ACTIONS.

Enterprising and progressive with the funds they handle, still they are found lending their influence to make the funds of the people ''unenterprising, slow, and inactive''.

Engaged in undertakings themselves, they warn the multitudes against them.

When a man is making money in business, he usually strives to conceal that fact from those around him; if others ask if there is an opening in his particular line, you may count on his giving a very pessimistic review of it.

Why should men with unlimited credit facilities for loans at banks, life insurance companies and other fiscal institutions seek to keep the money away from those institutions by preaching enterprise in lieu of thrift?

As they preach thrift, money pours in that they may use. Why should they go against their own interests? The answer, of course, is that they don't. They are not pushing a propaganda that would empty their financial reservoirs, but are preaching one that keeps them comfortably full.

Can you blame them?

"We live in an age that hath more need of good example than precepts", says George Herbert.

And Talleyrand says: "Society is divided into two classes: the shearers and the shorn. We should always be with the former against the latter."

The shearers capitalize the fact stated by Dillon, when he said: "The multitude are always in the wrong." Father is advised to deny himself tobacco, mother to forego some simple pleasure that would brighten her life, to further the magic thing termed "thrift".

As Swift said: "The stoical scheme of supplying our wants by lopping off our desires is like cutting off our feet when we want shoes."

Yet millions are engaged in precisely this

kind of thing under the insistent, persistent suggestion of "save, save, save".

Before the shearers can shear the profit off the dollar sheep, they must make the "unenterprising, dull, inactive, slow", stupid and timid little lambs jump as the others jump, whether there is any necessity to jump or not, until they are shepherded into the saving pens to be relieved of their financial wool and kept there by the force of habit, which, as Victor Hugo has well said, "is the nursery of errors".

"It requires a great deal of boldness and a great deal of caution to make a great fortune", is the dictum of Rothschild, perhaps the world's greatest financier.

If our ship is eventually to come home—if our legacy is to come from the future as our birthright—we must realize one big fact, the fact expressed by Rothschild, and that is that an element of speculation enters into every investment, and that an element of investment enters into every speculation; and, as we march forward, we must be prepared to exhibit in turn the qualities of boldness and caution which these two elements demand.

Interest represents a sum paid for the USE of money; and we must recognize the fact that if others can pay for what we have and make a profit, we can use what we have and make the profit they would make.

If we buy kine, and the kine breed, we must demand the progeny.

We must recognize three axioms, namely—

1. That the best preparation for the future is the present well seen to.

2. That work is the means of living, but it is not a living.

3. That wishes, like castles in the air, are inexpensive and not taxable.

Then—

We will begin the work of financial aggrandizement today and every other day.

We will work till our money works for us.

We will harness the wish to ACTION, and make it a concrete real thing.

In short, we will change our mental habits, "that nursery of errors", and graduate from the sheared to the shearing class.

If these lessons get you on that side of the fence, their preparation will not have been in vain.

"Union gives strength to, the humble", said Cyrus.

We have resolved to make our timid dollars enterprising and active. We have resolved to make them work—FOR US (because all dollars work—the capitalists see to that, if they are not buried under the hearthstone), and we must see to it that in the first flush of enthusiasm in our new role we do not become too INDIVID UALISTIC.

Dollars, like everything else, work best in droves; and in every activity of life or money, unity gives strength.

The big, profitable, unusual things—the real opportunities—take more money to "swing" than the average individual has.

So, to reap the benefit of them, a number of individuals must club their dollars together and own or control the opportunity that is offered.

This is done through the corporate device, which legally enables a number of individuals to operate together without the disadvantages of partnership, but with all its advantages.

But here we must learn that there are corporations and corporations; there is the coöperative corporation and the capitalistic corporation; the first gives you back the net earnings of your money, while the last gives you back a fraction of those net earnings.

How are we to know one from the other? Simply by observing the class of investment they offer us. The capitalistic corporation will offer either bonds, paying a fixed interest for the USE of our money, or shares of stock paying a FIXED dividend. No matter what the money paid for the bonds EARNS, we receive but a minimum portion of it. No matter what the money paid for the stock EARNS, we receive but a minimum portion of it.

The capitalistic corporation is nothing but the savings bank idea extended a little further, with bond buyers or preferred stockholders as depositors, and the capitalists as real shareholders.

We catch the distinction when we see the difference between what bank depositors get and what bank shareholders get. The First National Bank, for instance, paid an annual dividend of 40 per cent in the same year that the Bowery Savings Bank and other savings institutions cut the rate of interest paid depositors from 4 to 3½ per cent.

On the other hand, the coöperative corporation has not pledged itself to money lenders by issuing bonds. It has not arbitrarily pledged certain profits by issuing preferred stock carrying fixed dividends—it has not done any of these things and doesn't propose to do them, profitable or unprofitable as they might be, simply because it conserves all its earnings for all its stockholders to be equally divided among all, less operating expenses to be equally borne by all, in exact proportion to their investment.

MAKING MONEY MAKE MONEY.

When you find a new enterprise represented by a young corporation that has not created preferred stock or bonds, but is offering common stock, that by its charter and under common law, MUST distribute net earnings with exact equality, then you find the ideal investment for your funds; provided, of course, that the management is honest, and the enterprise on which it is based is sound and profitable.

So long as all the increased wealth which modern progress brings, goes but to build up great fortunes, to increase luxury, and make sharper the contrast between the House of Have and the House of Want, progress is not real and cannot be permanent.—Henry George.

Such a corporation does not go far before its shares of stock acquire the value in the open market that they deserve and are entitled to; consequently your principal is not tied up, but becomes as liquid as that on deposit in a savings bank, because if necessary the shares of stock held can be sold and the sum originally deposited regained.

The shares of stock of the Fifth Avenue Bank, for instance, paid 250 per cent in 1907, 260 per cent in 1908, 225 per cent in 1909, etc., etc., and its shares of stock (par value $100) sold at $4,250 each in the open market.

DISCOURSE XX.

By this, and hundreds of examples that could be readily given, it will be seen that when a deposit is made in a bank, as a DEPOSITOR, it can be drawn out after a specified term, with a little interest added; but when money is deposited in a bank as a SHAREHOLDER, it can be drawn out after a period, PLUS AN ENORMOUS PREMIUM.

The same thing rules in the small private corporation. Of course the corporation represents a business enterprise, and, as we have seen, no business enterprise is free from a certain proportion of hazard.

In this connection the story of two friends is interesting. Their names are purposely withheld, but for the sake of clearness we will call one Mr. Active, and the other Mr. Passive.

Mr. Active had initiative. He was a constructive, compelling personality, and he went into business for himself. Mr. Passive worked for another man. Three years passed, and Active had played and lost; he was "broke", while Passive had quite a little "nest egg" saved up, and was drawing $30 weekly.

Again Mr. Active launched his bolt. Four years later he had again been worsted; again he was "broke". Passive, on the contrary, had money invested in bonds, and was drawing $40 a week as salary.

A third time Active failed. Passive was getting along well; his investments returned him some $400 annually, and his salary was $65.

The fourth time Active attempted he succeeded. Today Active is worth several millions, and Passive is a somewhat prosperous clerk who envies Active.

The moral of this is that fortune and love befriend the bold—in other words, the bold try often, if necessary, learn from failures, if failures come, master the "knack", and ultimately succeed. Nothing Smiles said was truer than when he stated:

"It is a mistake to suppose that men succeed through success; they much oftener succeed through failure".

And keep this great fact in mind:

A FEW WINNINGS COMPENSATE HIGHLY FOR MANY LOSINGS, SIMPLY BECAUSE MONEY, ONCE IT IS EMPLOYED RIGHTLY, HAS SUCH TREMENDOUS GENERATIVE POWER THAT IT MAY BE LITERALLY COMPARED TO AUSTRALIAN RABBITS WHICH OVERRUN THAT CONTINENT AS A RESULT OF HALF A DOZEN BROUGHT THERE LESS THAN HALF A CENTURY AGO.

Carefully bear this fact in mind: "It requires a great deal of BOLDNESS and a great deal of

CAUTION to make a large fortune." One must balance, not overbalance, the other. Be cautious and bold.

In the words of Juvenal:

"Dare to do something worthy of transportation and a prison, if you mean to be anybody."

To get a chance, TAKE ONE.

The great Johnson said: "It is the care of a very great part of mankind to conceal their indigence from the rest. They support themselves by temporary expedients, and every day is lost in contriving for tomorrow."

Isn't that so wonderfully true that it pictures the life of ninety-five out of a hundred men? Are they not working—not for the future, but for the immediate present—to pay THE BILLS THAT ACCRUE AT THE END OF THE WEEK? They are running on ice, losing today contriving for tomorrow. Why not escape the endless treadmill by making YOUR MONEY work for you? It will do a man's part if you will let it. Learn to use your money, and UNLEARN the HABIT that has fastened round your neck like an Old-Man-of-the-Sea of letting others use it.

Take the two, five or ten dollars that you can save and make them coöperate with the dollars of others to the end that an achievement worth while may be created in the world; don't let those pieces of silver metaphorically rust, but HUMANIZE them and set them digging gold, silver, copper or lead in the West, South or East, as the case may be; let them swing axes, fell trees, tow timber and delve for coal; let them build industries to produce things of use to mankind; let each stand as a driving power behind the elbow of a man for a day; get the real truth out of that saying of Carlyle's, "Whoever has sixpence is sovereign over all men—to the extent of that sixpence; commands cooks to feed him, philosophers to teach him, kings to mount guard over him—to the extent of sixpence", and thus "get next" to the real productivity of labor and opportunity.

A thousand resources cry aloud for development in this land of opportunity—a thousand inventive brains cry for financial aid—all have everything needed except the one thing, money. And that you control.

Respond with the boldness, progressiveness and energy of the typical man of enterprise, and reap the rewards that these dumbly eloquent potentialities offer—lift them from potentialities to actualities—crystalize them into existent THINGS that enrich and ennoble the world, and, properly utilized, give to society, to you and your fellowmen your birthright and heritage—health, wealth and happiness.

ADDENDUM.

GLOSSARY OF FINANCIAL TERMS.

Above par. Higher than the par value.

Account and risk. Broker acts only as client's agent at the client's risk.

Account of sales. A broker's statement of purchases and sales for a client.

Accrued dividend. A dividend that is due but has not been paid.

Accumulated dividends. Dividends that are due but have not been paid.

Accumulative dividends. Preferred shares may be made to draw accumulative dividends. If the dividends on such shares are not paid, they must be paid in full to date before dividends may be paid on the common shares.

Active security. A stock or bond for which there is great demand—of which sales are made frequently.

Adjustment bond. Issued to raise money to adjust the finances of the company.

Allotment. A block of stock set aside for a specific purpose, or to be sold at a specified price.

Amortization. Providing a sinking fund for paying obligations due or to become due.

Assented. Depositing securities with an agreement consenting to a proposed change in the company.

Assess. Taxing stockholders a stated amount on each share to raise money needed by the company.

Assessment. A corporation's demand on its stockholders to pay into the treasury of the company a specified sum on each share of stock held.

Assets. Property available for paying debts.

Assign. Transferring ownership by writing.

Assign in blank. To transfer ownership of a stock certificate without naming the person to whom it is transferred.

At market. Buying or selling securities at the prevailing price.

At par. The face value of a share of stock or of a bond.

Averaging. Buying securities at a lower price after having bought at a higher. that the average cost of all may be lowered.

Bear. A stock exchange operator engaged in forcing down the prices of securities.

Bearing the market. Working to force down prices.

Below par. A price below the face value of a stock.

Bid. The price a buyer offers to pay for a security.

Bid and asked. Quotations of prices based on the day's transactions on the stock exchange.

Blanket mortgage. A mortgage covering several properties, or all the property of the one issuing the mortgage.

Blind pool. Persons contribute capital to a pool to operate on the exchange, and only one of them knows which security is to be operated in. The purpose is secrecy.

Block. A number of shares, as 100, 1,000, etc.

Bond. Certificate of obligation, secured by mortgage or otherwise, issued by a corporation, to pay money at a specified date.

Books close. At an advertised date a short time before a dividend is to be paid, the transferring of certificates of stock is stopped until after the dividend has been paid.

Books open. After a dividend has been paid the company's transfer books are opened and shareholders can again transfer their stock certificates.

Book value. Value of a stock based on the profits or deficit of a corporation as shown on its books.

Break. When the price of a stock falls suddenly. Happens usually when the "bulls" have kept up the price by artificial tactics.

Broker. One who executes buying and selling orders for the public.

Brokerage. Commission paid a broker for transacting business.

GLOSSARY

Bull. A stock exchange operator engaged in forcing up the prices of securities.

Bulling the market. Working to force up price.

Buy outright. Paying in full for stock purchased.

By-laws. Rules adopted by a corporation by which the transaction of its affairs is governed.

Call. The right by agreement to get a security in a stated time at a specified price.

Called bond. A bond carrying a clause giving the company that issued it the right to pay it at a fixed time and amount.

Call loan. Loan of money payable on demand.

Call money. Money borrowed subject to be paid back on demand.

Capitalization. Total amount of shares of stock of a company.

Cash assets. Cash on hand or in bank and securities immediately convertible into cash.

Certificate of stock. A certificate representing ownership of the stated number of shares in the company issuing the certificate.

Charter. The certificate that the state issues to a corporation giving it the right to do business.

Clique. Combination of operators to break or expand the market.

Close corporation. A corporation in which the stock is held by a few persons and public reports are not made.

Code. Compilation of words, each signifying a phrase, sentence, etc., used in sending telegrams and cables economically.

Collateral. Securities pledged for the payment of a loan.

Collateral trust bond. Has securities of other companies pledged with a trustee for its payment.

Common stock. Is not limited in the amount of dividends it may draw, and has no preference in the assets.

Consolidated bond. Issued to take up two or more outstanding bond issues. A renewal bond.

Continued bond. A bond on which interest does not stop at maturity. May be held indefinitely.

Convertible bond. May be exchanged for stock in the company at a specified time and price.

Corner. Control of the floating supply of a stock or commodity.

Coupon. A small certificate attached to a bond calling for the payment of a period's interest.

Coupon bond. Usually payable to bearer, with coupons attached calling for the payment of interest when due.

Covering. Buying stocks later to deliver on sales previously sold ''short''.

Cumulative dividend. When the dividend is cumulative and dividends remain unpaid, the back dividends must be paid before the current dividend can be paid.

Curb market. An exchange originally held in the street for buying and selling securities not listed on the stock exchange.

Current assets. Assets subject to change from day to day, such as cash on hand, etc.

Cutting a melon. Giving the stokcholders extra profit in the form of stock or cash.

Dabbling. Speculating a little now and then.

Deal. Secret agreement by a combination of men to depress or advance the price of a stock or group of stocks.

Debenture bond. A promise to pay, without the mortgage features.

Default. Failure to pay interest or principal.

Deferred bond. Interest deferred for a specified time.

Deferred dividends. Unpaid dividends on preferred shares that must be paid before dividends may be paid on common shares.

Deferred shares. Stock of a corporation on which dividends are not to be paid until some contingent condition arises.

Delivery. Physical delivery of a properly transferred stock certificate.

GLOSSARY

Depository. Financial institution in which money is deposited.

Digested securities. Indicating that more than one security has been issued, and that the public has bought all issues.

Direct liability. A liability definitely fixed—amount not dependent on contingencies.

Discretionary order. Giving the broker the right to use his discretion in filling an order.

Discretionary pool. One in which the operations of the pool are left to the discretion of one or more of its members.

Dividend. Stockholder's share of the divided profits of a corporation.

Divisional bond. Secured by a mortgage on a specified division of a railroad.

Domestic corporation. One doing business in the state in which it is incorporated.

Drawn bonds. Selected by lot to be paid when a certain number fall due.

Drive. Attempt to force down prices.

Drop in the market. Sudden falling of prices.

Dummy. One who serves for the purpose of concealing the identity of another.

Equipment. Engines and other rolling stock of a railroad. Buildings and machinery of a mine, etc.

Equipment bond. Secured by a lien on the equipment.

Equity. Difference between the market value of a security and the amount loaned on it.

Escrow. Putting a document or security in a third person's hands to be held until a specified condition has been met; the writing containing the escrow agreement.

Ex-Coupon. Describes a bond from which the coupon for the interest for the current period has been detached.

Ex-Dividend. Describes a stock sold while the transfer books are closed to pay dividends. Without the current dividend.

Ex-Drawing. Sale of a bond without any advantage the purchaser may have if it is drawn for redemption.

Ex-Rights. Sold without the option of the original holder to subscribe to new issues.

Extended bond. Original time of maturity extended.

Extension bond. Issued by a railroad to get money with which to extend its lines.

Finance. Science of the profitable management of money. Monetary affairs.

Financial statement. Tabular statement giving assets and liabilities, showing the financial condition of the company

First mortgage. Takes precedence over other mortgages Has first lien on the property.

First-mortgage bond. Secured by first mortgage.

Fiscal agent. Corporation's agent for the sale of its securities.

Fiscal year. The financial year of a government or company. The period between the annual balancing of its books.

Fixed capital. Permanent property, as lands and plant.

Flat. Without interest.

Floating debt. Unfunded indebtedness of a state or corporation.

Flurry. Sudden and severe decline in the market, accompanied by excitement.

Flyer. Speculative purchase of an occasional lot of shares for quick profit or loss.

Floating bonds. Selling an issue of bonds.

Floating stock. Selling an issue of stock.

For the account of. Broker's transactions for another.

Fractional orders or lots. Units of speculation are 100 shares of stock, and 5,000 bushels of grain. Lesser amounts are called fractional.

Franchise. Privilege conferred by grant from a government or municipality to a corporation or an individual.

Frozen out. When a trader on margin is sold out because he does not make good impaired margins, he is said to be "frozen out".

Full-paid stock. Stock for which the company has received, in some form, the full amount of the par value.

GLOSSARY

Full stock. Par value $100.

Funded debt. Debts converted into a permanent loan, usually in the form of bonds with interest.

Funding. Changing a floating indebtedness into a funded debt.

Futures. Trades made for future delivery.

General mortgage. Covers all the property subject to any earlier mortgage.

General mortgage bond. Secured by a general mortgage.

Gilt-edge. High class. Very best.

Gold bond. Principal and interest payable in gold.

Governing committee. The men who direct the affairs of a corporation.

Government bonds. Interest bearing obligations of a government. Bonds issued by the government.

Gross earnings. Total earnings before expenses are deducted.

Guaranteed bond. Payment of principal and interest guaranteed.

Guaranteed stock. Dividends and sometimes the principal guaranteed.

Gunning a stock. To make every effort to "break" the price when someone is a heavy holder of the stock and unable to withstand an attack. To force "longs" to sell, or "shorts" to buy.

Hedging. Buying other stocks to offset a possible loss on a stock sold "short".

Holding company. Does not operate, but owns the securities of other companies.

Holding the market. Distributing purchases skilfully in an attempt to keep up prices.

Honeycombed market. Prevalence of many "stop orders", meaning orders to sell when the price reaches a certain point, either up or down.

Hypothecation. Pledging securities or other personal property for the payment of borrowed money.

Income bond. Lien on net income of the corporation issuing the bond.

Incorporation price. The price paid the state for a charter for a corporation.

Indorsed bond. Non-registered coupon bond payable to bearer, containing owner's indorsement on it which does not properly belong on it.

Industrial stock. Shares in a corporation engaged in manufacture.

Inflated. Condition of a company having outstanding stock in excess of the value of the assets.

Initial dividend. First dividend declared by a company.

Improvement bond. Issued to get money to make improvements on the corporation's property.

Insiders. Men who own the controlling interest in a corporation and shape its policy.

Installment. Part of a debt due in payment of a security and payable at a specified time.

Interim dividend. Partial dividend made before the full dividend is ascertained and declared.

Investment. Money put into a company's shares to be held permanently for dividends. Opposite of buying for speculation.

Irish dividend. A wag's definition of an assessment on stocks.

Irredeemable bond. Can not be paid off, but continues to draw interest forever.

Irregular. A market in which some stocks advance while others decline.

Issue. Original delivery. Also the total amount of a security issued by a company.

Joint bid. Bid by two or more houses jointly. A partnership bid.

Joint bond. Principal and interest guaranteed jointly by two or more companies.

GLOSSARY

Joint mortgage. Covers the property of two or more persons or companies.

Kiting. Incurring a fresh obligation to discharge an old one. Usually done by having several bank accounts and depositing a worthless check ahead of overdrafts, and depositing another worthless check before the former worthless check is presented for payment and keeping up this practice until the depositor can deposit money to take care of the last worthless check.

Lamb. An inexperienced trader whom the experienced ones may easily "fleece".

Land-grant bond. Secured by a mortgage on a grant of land by the government to aid in development, such as building a railroad.

Legal investments. Securities in which banks, trust companies and insurance companies may legally invest the funds entrusted to them.

Liabilities. Obligations topay. What a company owes.

Lien. Any legal claim on a property.

Limited liability. Liability limited to the assets of the company.

Liquid assets. Cash and assets that may be quickly converted into cash.

Liquidation. Converting assets into cash. Also paying all obligations of a company preparatory to going out of business.

Listed securities. Stocks and bonds listed on a stock exchange that they may be sold and bought there.

Lloyds. An association of English underwriters of insurance, principally maritime.

Long. Carrying a lot of purchased stocks in anticipation of a rising market.

Manipulation. Forcing prices up or down for the purpose of selling or buying.

Margin. Money deposited with a broker to make good the purchase or sale of a stock.

Market price. The price that prevails at the moment the quotation is made.

Matched orders. Buying and selling orders on the same stock, matched in price, to show trading that prices may be influenced.

Milking the street. When an operator or a clique has a security so well in hand that he can alternately raise and lower the price and sell and buy to his advantage, taking all the money in sight, Wall Street is said to be "milked".

Mixed loan. Secured by collateral of different character.

Municipal bond. Issued by a political division having power to levy taxes, or by a subdivision of such a division.

Negotiable. May be transferred by delivery or assignment.

Net. What remains after all expenses have been paid.

Nominal. Existing in name only. No value.

Non-assented stocks or bonds. Owners refuse to assent to a reorganization of the company, and withhold their securities from deposit.

Non-assessable stock. Stock which may not be assessed.

Non-cumulative stock. Unpaid dividends do not accumulate to be paid later.

Odd lot. More or less than the regular unit of orders. In Wall Street 100 shares or $10,000 in bonds is a unit.

Open order. Good until cancelled.

Operating company. The company operating the business. The operating company's stock is owned by a holding company.

Option. A purchased privilege to buy or sell a security by a certain time at a specified price.

Optional bond. May be redeemed before maturity at the option of the company.

Overcapitalized. Having more capital than conditions warrant.

Overissue. A sale of more stock than has been authorized.

GLOSSARY

Over-the-counter. Selling stocks and bonds outside the exchange. Selling direct.

Paid-up stock. Stock fully paid for.

Paper profits. As they appear to be in transactions not yet closed.

Par. Face value.

Participating bond. It shares in profits, in addition to drawing interest.

Passing a dividend. Failing to pay a periodical dividend.

Passive bond. Draws no interest, but gives a special advantage, as a fixed income.

Pegged. A stationary market, neither rising nor falling.

Plain bond. Unsecured. Same as a promissory note.

Plant. Operating equipment.

Plunge. Buying heavily for speculation.

Point. One dollar of the price of a share of stock.

Pointer. A tip. Supposed accurate information about the future price of a security.

Pool. Several persons joining their money to do a specified thing in the hope of profits or other advantage.

Pounding. To sell freely, both long and short, with a view of changing prices.

Preferred stock. Draws specified dividends before dividends may be paid on the common stock.

Premium. The amount above par value.

Promoter. An organizer of a company.

Promoter's stock. Stock given a person for organizing a company.

Proprietary company. The company that owns or controls another.

Proxy. Power of attorney to represent and vote another's stock. Must be in writing.

Purchase money bond. Issued to get money to pay the purchase price of property.

Put. An agreement by which, for a consideration, one person acquires the right to deliver, or put, something to another at a fixed price in a specified time.

Pyramiding. Buying stock by using as margin the paper profits on stock already bought.

Quotation. The quoted or current price. Prices on stocks are usually quoted in eighths of 1 per cent.

Quarter stock. Par value $25.

Quick. Describes assets that may be quickly converted into cash.

Reaction. Fall in price.

Realize. To sell securities or other assets to get cash.

Realizing sale. To sell securities to secure profits.

Receiver. Temporary manager appointed by a court to take charge of a company's affairs and conserve them for the creditors.

Recovery. Advance in price after it has declined.

Redeem. To pay bonds at maturity.

Redeemable bond. May be called in and paid after a specified time.

Redeemable drawing. Deciding by lot which of the redeemable bonds are to be paid.

Refund. To take up outstanding securities by issuing others in their place.

Registered bond. Registered in the name of the owner, and transferrable by endorsement only.

Registered coupon bond. Principal payable to registered owner only, but interest coupons payable to bearer.

Registrar. Keeper of the record of the names of owners of the stock of a company.

Released indorsed bond. An indorsed bond bearing a certificate of release.

Reorganization. New organization to put a company on a better basis.

Repudiation. Rejecting a contract in whole or in part.

Retire. To pay off securities.

Resources. Available property of a company that may be turned into cash.

GLOSSARY

Rigging the market. Manipulating prices of stocks by insiders that the lambs may be "fleeced".

Scaled. In reorganizing, giving new securities of less value in exchange for the old. Reducing the amount of the outstanding securities.

Scalp. Buying and selling at a small profit.

Scrip. A certificate given for part payment on a stock, and redeemable when balance is paid.

Seasoned securities. Those on which many dividends or several periods of interest have been paid to indicate that their value is stable.

Second mortgage. Secured by property on which a first mortgage has been given.

Second mortgage bond. Secured by property on which a bond issue has already been made.

Serial bonds. Parts fall due at ends of designated successive periods.

Share. One of the equal parts of the capital stock.

Short. Having sold stock that the seller does not own.

Sight paper. Draft payable on demand.

Single maker paper. Bears the name of the maker only.

Sinking fund. A fund created and contributed to from time to time to pay an obligation at maturity.

Sinking fund mortgage. Payable from a sinking fund.

Slow assets. Property that requires time to be converted into cash.

Soft spot. Weak point in the market.

Special assessment bond. Payable by levying a special assessment on the property benefited by the money paid for the bonds.

Speculate. To buy securities with a view of selling at a higher price.

Split sale. Selling part of an order at one price and part at another.

Spread. Combining a call and put.

Squeeze. Advancing the price so those who sold short at a low price must pay a high price to deliver.

Stop loss. Order to sell at a loss if the price goes down to a given point.

Street. Term to designate the financial district of a city.

Surplus. Profit that remains after expenses and dividends have been paid.

Syndicate. A combination of capitalists.

Take up. To pay the balance due on a security purchased and receive the security.

Ticker. An electrical self-printing instrument installed in offices to print instantaneously the exchange quotations.

Time loan. Made for a specified time. Opposite of call loan.

Time money. Money loaned for a specified time.

Transfer. To put a security in the name of its new owner.

Transfer agent. Person delegated by a corporation to transfer its securities from one owner to another.

Treasury stock. The part of the corporation's stock held in the treasury, and which, when sold, brings money into the treasury for use by the company in its operations.

Trust. A combination of corporations pooling their businesses to gain some special advantage. Regularly it means holding property in trust for others.

Trust company. A financial house authorized by its charter to accept and execute trusts.

Trustee stock. Seasoned stock in which trustees are permitted by law to invest trust funds.

Underlying mortgage. A preceding mortgage.

Undertone. Describes the underlying strength or weakness of the market.

Underwriter. One who insures. One who guarantees to furnish a corporation a stated amount of money for a given amount of securities in a specified time.

Unfunded debt. Running debts that are not secured.

Unlisted. Describes securities that have not been listed on the stock exchange; securities that cannot be bought or sold on the exchange.

GLOSSARY

Unloading. Selling out a stock that has been held a long time.

Voting trust. Committee to whom is given the power to vote the controlling stock in a corporation to insure unity and control.

Wash sales. When one broker arranges with another to buy fictitiously at a price what the other offers, that the stock may have the record of having been bought and sold on the exchange, the sales are called wash sales. Stock exchange rules forbid such sales, but—

Watered stock. An increase in the capital stock without a corresponding increase in the company's assets.

When issued. Proposed stock to be delivered as soon as issued by the company.

Wind. Bears selling short what they haven't got, are said to sell wind.

Wiped out. Loss of margins. Same as "frozen out".

Working capital. Money used actively in conducting the company's business.

X-d. Ex-dividend.

X-i. Ex-interest.

Yield. The percentage of net profit that an investment returns.

Printed in the USA
CPSIA information can be obtained
at www.ICGtesting.com
LVHW082242090624
782786LV00011B/560

9 780766 160453